Garland
Studies
in

AMERICAN
INDIAN
LINGUISTICS

A series of ten monographs containing
the results of some of the most
significant recent research in the field.

A Grammar
of
Biloxi

Paula Ferris Einaudi

Garland Publishing, Inc., New York & London

1976

Library of Congress Cataloging in Publication Data

Einaudi, Paula Ferris.
   A grammar of Biloxi.

   (Garland studies in American Indian linguistics)
   Originally presented as the author's thesis, Uni-
versity of Colorado, 1974.
   Bibliography: p.
   1. Biloxi language--Grammar. I. Title.
II. Series.
PM702.E4 1976   497'.5   75-25114
ISBN 0-8240-1965-2

Printed in the United States of America

TABLE OF CONTENTS

ACKNOWLEDGMENTS

This research was originally prepared as my Ph. D. dissertation, which was completed in the spring of 1974 at the University of Colorado in Boulder. My advisor was Allan R. Taylor, who saw me through from the very tedious times of card filing to the relatively exciting days of the final draft and the defense. He was always generous with his time and perceptive in reading the various drafts I prepared for him. His optimism, his sense of humor, and particularly his deep knowledge of Siouan all made my task easier and more pleasant.

David S. Rood was also of great help; his careful reading of the quasi-final draft revealed numerous inconsistencies that I was glad to be able to correct before it was too late.

No one could ask for a better typist than Jeanette Trebing. A real pleasure to work with, she was fast and accurate, particularly considering the difficult material with which she had to work.

Alice Levine helped me with the proofreading; her experience in this field made this phase of the work much easier. She has my endless thanks for her time and judgment.

Beth Berry will always have a special place in my heart; without her unique help, combined with her enthusiasm and generosity, I might still be on Chapter One.

And finally, thanks go to my husband, Franco, and to my many friends whose encouragement and confidence gave me the strength to reach a long sought goal.

000. Introduction

Biloxi is a member of the Southeastern branch of Siouan along with Ofo and Tutelo (Haas 1968:84). It was first discovered to be Siouan by Alfred S. Gatschet in 1886 after very little field work. As he wrote to the Director of the Bureau of Ethnology:

> During the few days of my presence here (Lecompte, Rapides Parish, La.), I have had the good fortune of discovering two languages unknown to science up to the present: the Biloxi and the Tuni'hka... I do not hesitate to declare the former to be a Dakota dialect and you will see this confirmed by the extract below... (Gatschet: Oct. 24, 1886:1)

It was not quite true that Biloxi was 'unknown' before that: James O. Dorsey (1893:268) says that previously it was supposed to belong to the 'Muskhogean stock', and Haas (1969:286) says that it was considered an independent stock. Nonetheless, Gatschet's discovery was an important one, and solid linguistic knowledge on Biloxi can be said to date from 1886.

Geographically, the Biloxi were first reported to be on Biloxi Bay, Mississippi, in the mid-17th century. The French historian Margry (De couvertes, IV, 172) reported that they were on the Pascoboula River, about 40 miles further east, by 1699. In the 18th century they settled in central Louisiana, first in Avoyelles Parish and then in Bayou Rapides, near Alexandria.

By the early 19th century, there were only about 30 Biloxi left in Louisiana. Dorsey reports that according to the Sociedad Mexicana Geográfica (1870), there were also about 20 Biloxi families living on the east bank of the Neches River, in southeast Texas.

By the time Dorsey did his field work in 1892 and 1893, there were no more Biloxis in Avoyelles Parish, Louisiana; the few surviving members of the tribe were in nearby Lecompte, Rapides Parish. The last speaker of Biloxi was in her late 80's when Mary Haas and Morris Swadesh discovered her in 1934.

Dorsey's two trips to Louisiana (Jan.-Feb., 1892, and Feb. 1893) resulted in a respectable amount of material: 31 texts with both interlinear and free translations, as well as 50 pages of separately elicited utterances. Dorsey worked extensively on this material and had 5,000 entries of words for a Biloxi-English dictionary before he died in 1895. John R. Swanton took over the project of organizing the material, and in 1912 the texts, utterances, and dictionary were published as part of Bulletin 47 of the Bureau of American Ethnology. This Dictionary of the Biloxi and Ofo Languages has been the main source of information on Biloxi ever since.

In the ensuing years, Carl Voegelin (1939 and 1941), Hans Wolff (1950), G. Hubert Matthews (1958), and Mary Haas (1968 and 1969) have all published on Biloxi, although only Haas and Swadesh have used material other than the <u>Dictionary</u>. For the present analysis of Biloxi, Dorsey's texts, elicited utterances and dictionary entries serve as the bulk of the corpus. In addition, I have also used most of the articles, letters, jottings, etc. available on Biloxi at the Smithsonian Institution. Some of these were very useful; others were not. The bibliography on pages 4-10 may help others to separate the useful from the rest.

Writing a grammar of any language is an important linguistic endeavor, I think, because it will add to our knowledge of the languages of the world. But the main reason I decided to write a grammar of Biloxi was to synthesize Dorsey's data, and to get it into a form where it could be used by other Siouanists for comparative work. There has been some solid headway made on Proto-Siouan (notably by Wolff and Matthews), but since every fragment of Siouan material is of potential importance, every effort must be made to be as complete as possible. It is hoped that the following grammar of Biloxi will be a step in that direction.

050. Bibliography

The following is an annotated list of the material available on Biloxi at the Smithsonian Institution in Washington. The Smithsonian catalog numbers are listed at the end of each entry. Items marked with an asterisk are those not seen by the author.

1. Dorsey, J. Owen.[n.d.] Biloxi and Hidatsa lexical comparisons. 3 pp. 4800:343.

A list of about 30 items cognate in the two languages.

2. _____. 1893.[*]Biloxi-English vocabulary. Approx. 500 slips. 4800:357.

Indexes lexical items in notebooks 4 and 5 (see 15 below).

3. _____. [n.d.] Biloxi grammatical notes. 4 pp. 4800:353.

Miscellaneous verbal conjugations. Contains information covered elsewhere.

4. _____. [n.d.] Biloxi kinship groups. 7 pp. 4800:345.

An exhaustive list of 54 kin groups of Biloxi, inflected in each case in the 1st person singular. Dorsey also marks the groups that have cognate forms in other Siouan languages.

5. _____. [n.d.] Biloxi kinship terms. 4 pp. 4800:345.

Almost identical to 4 above, although it does not contain the information on cognates.

6. _____. [n.d.] Biloxi linguistic notes. Approx. 75 pages and slips. 4800:341.

Deals mostly with verbs, and seems to contain material present elsewhere. Unarranged, hard-to-follow, often illegible.

7. _____. [n.d.] Biloxi linguistic notes and texts. Approx. 93 pages. 4800:351

Labelled by Dorsey, "Biloxi notes which have been copied on slips for the Biloxi-English Dictionary." This is fortunate since the entire document is illegible. Dorsey must have crossed out each item here as he copied it onto other slips.

8. _____. [n.d.] Biloxi onomatology. 2 pp. 4800:349.

Very short and incomplete, although it contains some noteworthy information on derivation.

9. _____. [n.d.] Biloxi phonology with notes on comparative Siouan. 6 pp. 4800:339.

Alphabet used for recording Biloxi. Identical to pp. 271-274 of Dorsey (1893).

10. _____. 1893. *Biloxi texts, with interlinear translations. Approx. 150 pp. 4800:338.

Printed in Dorsey and Swanton (1912).

11. _____. [n. d.] Biloxi transitions. 13 pp. 4800:344.

A very good synopsis of pronominal relationships: 'he loves her, you love her, I love her; he loves them, you love them, I love them', etc. Typed, clear, easy-to-follow.

12. _____. 1884. Biloxi Verbal endings in 'ai-a'. 3 pp.

A very curious item, since there are no verbs in Biloxi that end in ai-a. This is labelled as part of a report made by Dorsey to the Director of the Bureau of Ethnology in 1884. This in itself is probably enough to prove that it is not Biloxi, since Dorsey had almost no information on Biloxi until two years later.

13. _____. [n. d.] Biloxi verbs. 30 pp. 4800:342.

Very clear conjugation of many verbs. Dorsey outlines what he considers to be 14 separate conjugations and 35 verbs that were unclassifiable. A very poor job of analyzing the verbs from a modern viewpoint, but nevertheless very useful.

14. _____. 1892-93. Biloxi vocabulary and notes.
Rapides Parish, La., Jan. 21-Feb., 1892, Feb. 4-25,
1893. Approx. 100 pp. 4800:348.

Fairly extensive vocabulary; includes comments
regarding place names in the Rapides Parish, La. area,
animal and plant names, body parts, kin terms, tools, etc.
Also contains some verbal conjugations.

15. _____. 1892-1893. *Biloxi vocabulary, phrases
and miscellaneous notes, Lecompte, Rapides Parish, La.
Approx. 750 pp. in 5 notebooks. 4800:356.

16. _____. [n.d.] Gatschet's Biloxi vocabulary
compared with Siouan dialects. 2 pp. 4800:347.

Of little help, since Dorsey filled in cognate forms for
only 4 items.

17. _____. [n.d.] Notes on Biloxi phonology. 18 pp.
4800:340.

Quite disorganized and not very useful.

18. Dorsey, James Owen, and Swanton, John R. [n.d.] *Biloxi-
English dictionary. Approx. 3,155 cards. 4800:358.

Printer's copy for Dorsey and Swanton (1912), pp. 169-
318. Most of the cards are by Dorsey, with additions and
revisions by Swanton, including revision of the phonetic
symbols.

19. _____. 1892-1908. [*]Biloxi texts and phrases with interlinear and free translations and notes.

    Identical to Dorsey and Swanton (1912), pp. 1-167. 4800:354.

20. Gatschet, Albert S. 1886. Biloxi vocabulary. (collected Oct. -Nov., 1886) with some cognate forms in Catawba, Santee, Yankton and Teton Dakota, Hidatsa, Kansas, and Tutelo. 8 pp. 933-b.

    A basic vocabulary. Clear, easy-to-read. Given its nature, there is little here that is not in the dictionary. Good as a check on Dorsey's forms, however, and includes many cognates from other Siouan languages.

21. _____. [n. d.] Biloxi vocabulary, recorded in 1886. 17 pp. 3436.

    This peculiar list is copied on Smithsonian Institution Comparative Vocabulary form 170, and thus contains cognate forms in French, English, Spanish, and Latin. Gatschet has added in his own writing the forms from Biloxi, Chilkat (Tlingit), Chilean, and Allentiac (also called Huarpe or Guarpe, an extinct South American isolate which is possibly related to Arancanian).

22. _____. Oct. 24, 1886. Letter to the director of the Bureau of Ethnology, announcing the discovery of the Biloxi and Tunica languages, and enclosing brief vocabularies. Lecompte, Rapides Parish, La. 7 pp. 1347.

Interesting, and of obvious value in the history of the classification of North American Indian languages.

23. _____. Oct.-Nov., 1886. Words and sentences of the Biloxi language. Lecompte, Rapides Parish, La. 68 pp. 933a.

Useful, although it contains a good deal of information available elsewhere. It is always interesting, however, to compare Gatschet's forms to Dorsey's:

1. What Dorsey writes as ⱡ (ṭ in the <u>Dictionary</u>), Gatschet renders as d:

   Dor. ṭopi = Gat. dopi   'young'

2. Dorsey's ⱦ (ḳ in <u>Dict.</u>) = Gat. g:

   Dor. yinḳóⁿni = Gat. yingóni   'married man'

3. Gatschet often hears initial /h/ where Dorsey hears nothing:

   Gat. hiptcóne = Dor. iptcone   'your nose'

4. Gatschet hears far fewer nasal vowels than Dorsey:

   Gat. háxti = Dor. áⁿxti   'woman'

The following articles are also available at the Smithsonian Institution. They are listed separately because they contain no linguistic information.

1. Dorsey, James Owen. [n.d.] Biloxi myths. 8 pp. 4800:350.

    These are abstracts, and according to the Smithsonian, probably intended for publication in JAFL.

2. _____. [n.d.] Historical sketch of the Biloxi. 6 pp. 4800:346.

    Identical to Dorsey (1893), pp. 267-271.

3. Porter, Kenneth W. Jan. 3, 1944. Letter to John R. Swanton, enclosing an account of Biloxi history based on field work in Texas and Mexico. Vassar College, Poughkeepsie, New York. 7 pp. 4195.

4. Speck, Frank G. [n.d.] Note on the location of the Biloxi Indians. 1 p. 4231.

The following articles represent the major published sources of information on Biloxi:

1. Dorsey, James O. 1893. The Biloxi Indians of Louisiana. Proceedings of the American Association for the Advancement of Science. 43, 267-287.

    Contains a short historical sketch of the Biloxi, as well as a brief grammar.

2. Dorsey, James O. and Swanton, John R. 1912. A
Dictionary of the Biloxi and Ofo Languages. BBAE 47.
Washington.

The basic source of information on Biloxi.

3. Haas, Mary R. 1968. The last words of Biloxi. IJAL 34.
77-84.

An account of field work done by Haas and Swadesh in
1934 with the last known speaker of Biloxi, Mrs. Emma
Jackson. Contains a comparison of their forms with
Dorsey's, followed by a phonemic analysis of Biloxi, and
reconstructions of Ohio Valley Siouan (Biloxi, Ofo and
Tutelo) which she proposes to rename Southeastern Siouan.

4. Haas, Mary R. 1969. Swanton and the Biloxi and Ofo
Dictionaries. IJAL 35. 286-90.

Points out the difficulties of working with Dorsey's
dictionary, and consequently how many people (e. g.
Matthews and Wolff) have overlooked or misinterpreted
information which it contains.

5. Matthews, G. Hubert. 1958. Handbook of Siouan Languages.
University of Pennsylvania dissertation (Ms.).

Contains much information in Biloxi, but also leaves
much unsaid, due to the difficulties pointed out in Haas
(1969). Contains also innumerable typing errors, skipped

lines, omitted charts, etc. , making it a difficult manuscript to follow.

6.   Voegelin, C. F.   1939.   Ofo-Biloxi sound correspondences. Proceedings of the Indiana Academy of Science. 48. 23-26.

Shows how Biloxi and Ofo are closer to one another than they are to Tutelo.   Also claims that of the two, Ofo contains more archaic forms.

7.   _____. 1941.   Internal relationships of Siouan languages. AA 43. 246-249.

Shows how Biloxi, Ofo,and Tutelo all form their own group within Siouan, which he proposes to call Ohio Valley Siouan.

8.   Wolff, Hans. 1950, 1951.   Comparative Siouan I, II, III, IV. IJAL 26. 61-66, 113-21, 168-78; 27. 197-204.

The most comprehensive treatment to date of Proto-Siouan.

Note

Almost every example of Biloxi in this thesis is accompanied by a page reference.   The large majority of these comes from Dorsey and Swanton (1912).   When both the page and line are indicated (e. g. 135-21), the quote comes from either a text or from the elicited utterances.   If the reference is to a page and column (e. g. 178a), it means that the information was obtained from the dictionary. References beginning with 4800: indicate one of the Smithsonian documents; individual articles and page numbers are also given with these references.

There are a few examples that are not accompanied by page references; these are one word entries, however, and can be found simply in the dictionary.

CHAPTER I

PHONOLOGY

100. Introduction

110. In his Vice-Presidential address to the American Association for the Advancement of Science, Dorsey gave a list of the
graphs which he used for writing Biloxi. These are as follows:

a, ă, â, b, c, d, dᶠ, e, ě, f, g, h, ꭒ, i, ĭ, j, k, ꓵ, l, m, n, ñ,
⁻ⁿ, o, p, d̶, q, r, s, t, ꝗ, tˤ, u, ŭ, û, u̱, w, y

John R. Swanton did considerable editing of Dorsey's work, and in
preparing the Dictionary (1912), he changed some of Dorsey's
graphs. His transcriptional system is as follows:

a, a̱, â, ă, b, c, d, d¢, dj, e, ě, ē, ê, f, g, h, i, ĭ, ī, j, k, x,
x̣, ḵ, l, m, n, ñ, ⁻ⁿ, o, ō, p, p̣, r, s, t, ṭ, tc, tç, u, û, ŭ, ū, u̱,
ü, w, y

Judging from Swanton's description of these sounds, and
taking into consideration also J. W. Powell's 1880 proposals for
an alphabet to be used in working with American Indian languages[1],

_____

[1] John Wesley Powell. 1880. Introduction to the Study of
Indian Languages. 1-16. Washington.

I assume that these graphs have approximately the following
phonetic values:

	labial	dental	mid-palatal	velar	post-velar
stops					
vls.	p	t	c (tc)	k	
med. vce.	ᵽ	ṭ		ḳ	
vd.	b	d	j (dj)	g	
affricates		t^{θ} (tç)			
		$d^{\eth}$ (dȼ)			
fricatives	f	s	š (c)	x, x̣,	
			ź (j)		
nasals	m	n		ŋ	
laterals		r			
		l			
glides	w		y		h

vowels

front		back
i, ī		u, ū
I (ǐ)	ə (ạ, û, ǔ)	U (û)
e, ē	ʌ (ǔ)	o, ō
ɛ (ê, ě)		
æ (ǎ)		ɔ (â)
a, ā		

+nasalization

120. Anyone who has worked at all with the Dorsey/Swanton texts will realize that the above list is far too extensive. Indeed, Dorsey himself pointed out the marginal value of the following phones: (Dorsey and Swanton 1912: 2):

b   occurs only once, in a proper name

d   rarely used (see t and t)

f   rarely used, and then owing probably to faulty hearing

g   as in go, seldom heard

1   occurs only in two modern names

r   occurs in one proper name

It is puzzling that Dorsey claimed that [d] is 'rarely used', since it is a very common graph throughout the corpus. This characterization cannot be an oversight since he mentioned it both here and in his Vice-Presidential address (1893: 271), and since in both cases he added '(see t and ṭ)'. I assume that he is here referring to the endless number of cases in which [d] seems to alternate freely with [t] and [ṭ], e.g. topi ~ dopi ~ atopi, 'new'. All of this seems to point to a sizeable amount of mishearing on Dorsey's part together with a lack of normalization.

130. G. Hubert Matthews recognized these shortcomings and postulated the following phonemic analysis for Biloxi based on Dorsey's corpus (1958: 12):

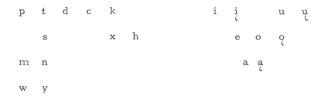

p t d c k   i i̧   u u̧

s   x h   e o o̧

m n   a a̧

w y

Besides collapsing the stops into a single series, and eliminating the marginal consonants, the most obvious change Matthews made was to propose nasal vowels instead of Dorsey's [⁻ⁿ] and [ñ]. In addition, he suggested that what Dorsey wrote as û or ŭ/__k should actually be rendered as [a]. Of course, these differences represented no basic change in the system, but only a change in representation. Nonetheless, it was a fundamental step forward in normalizing Biloxi phonology.

Matthews' analysis seems accurate, except for his postulation of both /o̧/ and /u̧/. /o̧/ occurs in the corpus far more than /u̧/, and almost all entries showing /u̧/ have variant forms with /o̧/, e. g. oⁿni ~ uⁿni, 'mother'. I therefore would posit only three phonemic nasal vowels: /i̧/, /a̧/, and /o̧/.

140. Mary Haas gave the following phonemic inventory for Biloxi, based on her own brief field work on the language (1968: 80):

p t č k   i i̧   u

   d   e ə o̧ o

   s x h   a a̧

m n   + length for all vowels except /ə/

w y

of marginal status:

b

f (ɸ̣)

š

As can be seen easily, Haas gives marginal status to /b/, /f/, and /š/, whereas Matthews did not include them at all. She also posits three nasal vowels instead of four, and includes /ə / and vowel length which Matthews did not. Haas' inventory seems to me the preferable one, and I will be following it throughout the dissertation with the minimal substitution of /c/ for /č/.

141.   The following comparative list shows the differences between the Dorsey, Swanton and Haas transcriptions of Biloxi. Page references are for Dorsey (1893), Dorsey-Swanton (1912) and Haas (1968).

Dorsey	Swanton	Haas	
tohoqka 276	tohoxka 278a	təho(·)xka 79b	'horse'
tcuñx̌i 276	tcuñx̣i 267b	čǫki 79a	'dog'
ayeki 281	ayeki 291b	əye·ki 78b	'corn'
a^{n}qti 279	a^{n}xtí 177b	ąxti 80b	'woman'
kcicka, kciqka 283	kcicka, kcixka 213b	kšixka 79b	'hog'
qkǐdédi 277	xx̣ǐdédi 182b	xkide·di 79a	'I'm going home'
a^{n}yadi 267	a^{n}yádi 179a	ąya·di 7 9b	'person' (with ꞥ, -di)
ita 270	itá 268a	ita· 785	'deer'
anahi^n 275	ánahi^n 172b	ana#hį 79a	'human hair'
ayepi 273	ǎyepi 176b	əyepi 79a	'door'
tckuyĕ 274	tckuyé 265b	čku·ye 80b	'sweet'

150. There are two points which Haas makes, however, that I
have not been able to verify from the corpus. The first concerns
vowel length. Since she actually heard Biloxi spoken, we must
take her word for its existence. Dorsey unfortunately is far too
erratic in his rendering of length for us to make any firm conclusions about it. For example, a brief look at the /a-/ entries in
the dictionary reveals the following discrepancies:

ade, ade, 'burn'

ahi, ahé, ahě, 'skin'

akidi, akĭdi, 'insects'

axokí, axók, axóg, axokya^n, 'canes'

anísti, anísti, 'sure enough'

atxe, atxe, 'ice, frozen'

atŭksé, adukšě, atkse, 'cover, lid'

ạyepi, ayéwi, 'door'.

The second point concerns the existence of /ə/. Judging
from the Dorsey/Swanton descriptions of English equivalents
["ạ as in final, û as in foot, ŭ as in but" (Dorsey-Swanton 1912:2),
I think Dorsey probably heard a [ə]. However, he has used at
least three graphs for it, and sometimes gives alternating forms
including a lengthened form of the same vowel, e.g. tụtúxka ~
tŭduxká, 'short'. In addition he has not always heard [ə] where
Haas has, e.g. 'horse' above. It thus seems almost impossible
to come to any firm conclusions about it, and I have therefore

decided to normalize as follows: D/S a = a; D/S û, ŭ = u. Readers
are advised to check D/S for the original citations regarding /ə /
as well as length and stress.

160. Dorsey is as inconsistent in his rendering of stress as he is
with length. For example:

a^{n}ya xohi   'old woman' 44-1

a^{n}yá xóhi   'old woman' 44-2

hú hakánaki   'he was coming out in sight' 62-28

hú akanáx   'he was coming out in sight' 95-239

hú ákanakí   'he came out in sight' 156-25

tĭdupí hánde   'he was alighting' 47-16

tĭdupi há   'he alighted, and' 90-123

tĭdúpi ha   'he came down, and' 92-169.

In view of the erratic transcriptions of length and stress, no
attempt will be made to deal with suprasegmental features.

170. Another problem in normalizing the Biloxi material has to
do with Dorsey's an and añ: it is often difficult to tell whether we
are dealing with /ą/ or /an/. Sometimes, as in mañki, 'he is
reclining', the morphophonemic alternations of the word indicate
that it was most likely /mąki/. In other cases, e.g. ande, 'he is',
there are no such morphophonemic clues to go on, and I have thus

had to make some admittedly arbitrary decisions in this regard.

Readers are again advised to check the original citations for /a̧/

and /an/.

200. In sum we will be using the following phonological inventory:

p	t	c	k		i	i̧			u
	d				e			o	o̧
	s		x				a	a̧	
m	n								
w		y	h						

Of marginal status:

b

f

š

210. The following minimal pairs support the above analysis:

p	pa	'head'
m	ma	'ground'
w	wa	'very'
t	ti	'house'
c	ci	'they lie down'
s	si	'yellow'

k	ka̧	'when'
x	xa̧	'where'
h	ha̧	'and'
t	tedi	'he is dead'
d	dedi	'he went'
d	de	'he went'
n	ne	'he stands'
m	ma̧ki	'he is lying down'
n	na̧ki	'he is sitting'
w	wahe	'he cries out'
y	yahe	'this'
w	wa	'very'
h	ha	'or'
i	ani	'water'
e	ane	'louse'
a	ha	'or'
u	hu	'he comes'
o	ko	'nominal particle'
u	ku	'he gives'

a	adi	'he climbed'
o	odi	'he shot'
i	kiya	'again'
u	kuya	'under'
i	ti	'house'
y	tyi	'medicine'
u	xudedike	'that way'
w	xwudike	'loosely'
i	ide	'it falls'
i̧	i̧de	'dung, manure'
a	da	'he gathers'
a̧	da̧	'he holds'
o	dohi	'anything rubbed or smeared'
o̧	do̧hi	'he sees'

300.   Phonotactics

310.   Biloxi allows the following consonant clusters[2]:

---

[2]Clusters including a juncture are not included here.

1st member \ 2nd member	p	t	d	c	k	s	x	h	m	n	w	y
p		x		x	x	x	x		?			
t	x				x	x	x	?		x	x	
d							?					
c	x	x			x							
k	x	x	x	x		x	x			x	x	x
s	x	x	x	x	x				x			
x	x	x	x	x	x					x	x	
h												
m												
n		x	x		?	x					x	
w												
y												

x = clusters verified

? = clusters attested in rare and/or suspect examples

320. Based on the above chart, we can make the following observations about consonant clusters:

1. C_1C_1 never occurs.

2. While /d/ is a very common phoneme, there is only one example of it as the first member of a cluster, and that example is itself suspect. On the other hand, it often

appears as a second member of a cluster, making its patterning more like that of a sonorant than of an obstruent.

3. With the exception of n + C, sonorants are never the first members of clusters, and never combine with other sonorants.

4. With the exception of 2 suspect examples, /h/ and /m/ never appear as the 2nd member of clusters.

5. Two fricatives never appear together.

330. Examples of these clusters are as follows:

p	t	akiptaye	'she caught both in one hand'
	k	kdopka	'deep dish or soup plate'
	c	pcǫ	'nose'
	s	psi	'night'
	x	pxidi	'he cheats'
	n	ạpni	' something worn from the neck'
			(also attested: ạpuni)
t	p	tpạhį	'any soft part of the body'
	k	tkana	'peaches'
	s	tsipa	'100'
	x	txoki	'toadstool'
	m	tmocka	'wildcat'
	w	putwi	'it crumbles off'
	y	tyi	'medicine'

d	h	hadhi	'he begs' (not in a text; provenience unknown)
c	p	įcpe	'he laughs at him'
	t	cti	'red'
	k	ckane	'nine'
k	p	yuȼpe	'his or her legs'
	t	ȼtu	'cat'
	d	ȼdexi	'spotted'
	c	ȼca	'he chops'
	s	ȼsedi	'he breaks'
	x	haȼxidi	'he gets angry'
	n	įȼne	'he vomits'
	w	ȼwįhi	'valley'
	y	ȼyąhi	'he scolds'
s	p	įspe	'he knows how to'
	t	stąhį	'he cuts with scissors'
	d	pesdoti	'he plays on a flute'
	c	scuki	'it is tough'
	k	sȼuti	'deep'
	n	snihi	'it is cold'

x	p	doxpe	'coat'
	t	pixti	'she is very good'
	d	dixdo	'he hulls beans'
	c	yaxci cukǫni	'midriff'
	k	exka	'buzzard'
	w	xwitka	'muddy'
	y	xyepi	'shallow'

n	t	nanteke	'nearly'
	d	ande	'he is'
	s	nsuki	'squirrel'
	x	nxodohi	'species of garfish'
	y	apenyikyahayi	'goldfinch'

340. Further restrictions on segmental sequences.

Three consonant clusters are relatively rare in Biloxi. All of the examples verified in the corpus are either:

  a. C + s + stop or

  b. C + x + glide

In addition, some of these words are attested in alternate forms, with a vowel after the first or second consonant, e. g. pstuki ~ pastuki, ' she sews'.

The following is a list of all the three consonant clusters:

  pst pstuki ~ pastuki 'she sews'

  psd psdehi ~ psudehi 'knife' (also attested as spdehi)

tsp	atspạhi	'it adheres' (Gatschet:
		hadespapahi, 281a)
tsk	kutska ~ kudeska	'fly'
	ạtska	'infant'
kst	aksteke	'he is stingy'
nsk	apadenska	'butterfly'
pxw	pxwe ~ pxe	'he punches'
txy	akutxyi	'letter'
kxw	xoxo kxwehe	'he sits on a swing'
	ịkxwe	'always'
kxy	pukxyi	'loop'

350. The syllable canon seems to be as follows:

$$(C)(C)(C)V(C)$$

or $(C)V(C)(C)$

(The onsets and codas of syllables are based on what can occur initially and finally.)

From this it follows that:

a. Only one consonant cluster is allowed per syllable.

b. $\left.\begin{array}{l} V_1V_1 \\ \\ V_1V_2 \end{array}\right\}$ never occur in the same syllable.

c. Three consonant clusters may begin a syllable, but they never end a syllable.

351. Consonant clusters rarely end syllables. When they do, it is almost certainly a case of vowel deletion, e. g. <u>tohoxk</u> from <u>tohoxka</u>, 'horse'.

352. Almost all words end in a vowel. Of those that do not, most end in /k/ or /x/, and here, as with clusters, the examples are usually shortened forms, e. g. <u>tox</u> from <u>toho</u>, 'he fell'.

400. Morphophonemics

1.   There are numerous verb roots and two mode markers in Biloxi with an e~a~i alternation. This alternation is conditioned by the following morpheme. Morphophonemically, I represent these verbs as ending in ‖ E ‖ since /e/ occurs much more often than the others. The most common among these verbs are:

dE	'go'
tE	'die'
andE, yukE	'be'
uwE	'enter'
nondE	'throw away'
yE	'cause'
ksE	'break'
nE	'stand'
akuwE	'take along'
idE	'fall'

tucE   'touch'

picE   'leap'

ktE   'hit'

E   'say'

towE   'be full'

naxE   'hear'

xkE   'peel'

i̯spE   'know how to'

The mode markers are:

tE   'optative mode marker'

dandE   'potential mode marker'

The morphemes governing the alternations are as follows:

$\|E\| \to$ /a/ / ___ : $\|E\| \to$ /i/ / ___ : $\|E\| \to$ /e/ / elsewhere

hi, hortatory mode marker   xti, intensifier

dandE, potential mode marker

ni, negative imperative mode;

    embedded negative

    mode marker

∅, imperative mode marker

    (female to female)

te, imperative mode marker

    (female to male)

xo, subjunctive mode marker

$\|E\| \rightarrow /a//\underline{\quad}:$ $\qquad\qquad$ $\|E\| \rightarrow /i//\underline{\quad}:$ $\quad$ $\|E\| \rightarrow /e//$ elsewhere

na, strong negative imperative

$\quad$ mode marker

xa̧, ?

o̧, o̧ni, completive mode marker

Examples:

$\underline{\|E\| \rightarrow /a/}$

$\quad$ $\|$ adE + hi $\| \rightarrow$ /ada hi/ $\quad$ 'they will go' $\quad$ 75-69/70

$\quad$ $\|$ nk + dE + dandE $\| \rightarrow$ $\|$ nde + dandE $\|$ $\quad$ (16)

$\qquad\qquad\qquad$ $\rightarrow$ /nda dande/ $\quad$ 'I will go' $\quad$ 137-3

$\quad$ $\|$ dE + ni kiyuhi $\| \rightarrow$ /da ni kiyuhi/ $\quad$ 'he wished he would go

$\qquad\qquad\qquad$ (but he did not)' $\quad$ 163-2

$\quad$ $\|$ yukE + $\emptyset$ $\| \rightarrow$ /yuka/ $\quad$ 'you all stay here!' $\quad$ 157-29

$\quad$ $\|$ dE + te $\| \rightarrow$ /da te/ $\quad$ 'go!' $\quad$ (fem. to male) $\quad$ 46-12

$\quad$ $\|$ nk + ay + naxtE + xo $\| \rightarrow$ $\|$ nk + ay + naxta xo $\|$

$\qquad\qquad\qquad$ $\rightarrow$ /i̧naxta xo/ $\quad$ (21)

$\qquad\qquad\qquad$ 'I will kick you if...' $\quad$ 13-12

$\quad$ $\|$ ay + adE + na $\| \rightarrow$ $\|$ ay + ada na $\| \rightarrow$ /yada na/ $\quad$ (20)

$\qquad\qquad\qquad$ 'do not go!' $\quad$ (pl.) $\quad$ 112-8

$\quad$ $\|$ a̧yato nkandE + xa $\| \rightarrow$ /a̧yato nkanda xa/ $\quad$ 'I am a man'

$\qquad\qquad\qquad$ 160-8

$\quad$ $\|$ adE + o̧ni $\| \rightarrow$ /ada o̧ni/ $\quad$ 'they were going' $\quad$ (in the past)

$\qquad\qquad\qquad$ 68-19

$\underline{\|E\| \rightarrow /i/}:$

$\quad$ $\|$ ca yE + xti ande $\| \rightarrow$ /ca yixti ande/ $\quad$ 'he was killing all'

$\qquad\qquad$ 33-1

$\|E\| \rightarrow /e/$:

    $\| nk + dE + ni \|$ /nde ni/   'I did not go'   25-17

               (see Rule 16)

    $\| tąhi̧ \, dE + di \| \rightarrow$ /tąhi̧ de di/   'she went running'   92-153

    $\| adE + \# \| \rightarrow$ /ade/   'they went'   75-72

There is evidence that this e~a~i alternation once existed in the connective eke as well (see 950), although by the late 19th century it was clearly an unproductive rule. The following forms support this conclusion:

        eke   'well'

        eką̧   'well'

        ekahą̧   'and then'

        ekeką̧   'and then'

        ekiką̧   'whereupon'

2.   Nouns and verbs whose stems end in -Vhi or -Vhi̧ undergo the following changes when followed by the plural marker -tu

    1. $\left.\begin{array}{l} i \\ i̧ \end{array}\right\} \rightarrow \emptyset$

    2.   h → x

Examples:

    $\| ańahi̧ + tu \| \rightarrow$ /anaxtu/   'their hair'   172b

    $\| ay + ą̧hi̧ + tu \| \rightarrow$ /ayą̧xtu/   'you pl. cry'   177a

    $\| dǫhi + tu \| \rightarrow$ /dǫxtu/   'they see'   184b

‖ i̯hi̧ + tu‖ → /i̧xtu/   'they arrive'   197a

‖ i̯dahi + tu‖ → /i̧daxtu/   'they seek'   201b

‖ asa̧hi̧ + tu‖ → /asa̧xtu/   'their arms'   251b

‖ yuhi + tu‖ → /yuxtu/   'they think'   292a

‖ nk + duyuhi + tu‖ → ‖nk + duyuxtu‖ → /nduyuxtu/   (16)

'we shake off the fruit from the tree'   295a

2. 1   This rule is optional for the root <u>duti</u> 'eat' as well:

‖duti + tu‖→ /dutitu/ ∼ /duxtu/   'they eat'   31-5;

4800:342:10

2. 2   This same hi/hi̧ → h → x rule applies optionally in compounds and across word boundaries when the following element begins with CV:

‖ a̧ya + sahi + ti‖→ /a̧yasaxti/   'Indian house'   179b

‖ ayohi + keci‖→ /ayox keci/   'Crooked Lake'   207b

‖ asa̧hi̧ + no̧pa‖→ /asa̧x no̧pa/   'both arms'   251b

3.   Nouns ending in -<u>di</u> that are subject to pluralization (see 610) undergo the following changes:

1. i → ∅
2. d → x $\Big/$ _____ tu

Examples:

‖ adi + tu‖ → /axtu/   'their father'

∥dodi + tu∥ → /doxtu/   'their throats'

∥indi + tu∥ → /i̧xtu/   'they'

4.　　Verbs whose stems end in -Vki, -Vpi or -si optionally drop

the final -i before the plural marker -tu:

-Vki:

∥pastuki + tu∥ → /pastuktu/   'they sew'　142-6

∥duksuki + tu∥ → /duksuktu/   'they broke the cord by

pulling'　213a

∥nk + apsuki + tu∥ → /nkapsuktu/   'we surrounded'　248a

∥akipupsuki + tu∥ → /akipupsuktu/   'they intercepted it'

4800:342:3

But:

∥haiki + tu∥ → /haikitu/   'they are related'　4800:342:5

-Vpi:

∥daksupi + tu∥ → /daksuptu/   'they got the juice out by

chewing'　4800:342:8

∥duhapi + tu∥ → /duhaptu/   'they pulled it off her head'

4800:342:9

But:

∥nk + i̧pi + tu∥→　/nki̧pitu/   'we put down a large

horizontal object on something'　202b

-si:

∥dusi + tu∥ → /dustu/   'they grabbed'　254a

‖akidisi + tu‖ → /akidistu/   'they aid him'   (masc. stem)

4800:342:2

‖akitsi + tu‖ → /akitstu/   'they aid him'   (fem. stem)

4800:342:2

But:

‖ahi̜ + atsi + tu‖ → /ahi̜atsitu/   'they sell'   4800:342:4

‖misi + tu‖ → /misitu/   'they sneeze'   4800:342:17

5.   ‖k(i)‖ → x/___k   This rule applies across morpheme
boundaries as well as across word boundaries. It is always
optional.

Examples:

‖ay + nk + kiduwe‖ → ‖ya̜k + kiduwe‖   (24)

→ /ya̜xkiduwe/   'you untie me'   62-22

‖uxtaki ka̜‖ → /uxtax ka̜/   'when he pushed her'   93-177

‖akanaki ka̜‖ → /akanax ka̜/   'when he was coming in sight'

95-239

‖kuhik na̜ki ka̜‖ → /kuhik na̜x ka̜/   'when it was sitting high'

149-10

‖ma̜ki ka̜‖ → /ma̜x ka̜/   'when it was reclining'   149-11

The following example shows that this rule is optional:

‖ya̜k + kinita̜ + xti‖ → /ya̜kinita̜ xti/   (10)

'it is too large for me'   134-18

5.1   There are various instances where the nasalization of the previous vowel is lost after this rule:

$\|$ay + nk + kica daha$\|$ → $\|$yąk + kica daha$\|$ (24)

→ /yaxkica daha/

'you have not forgotten us'   21-2

$\|$mąki   kide$\|$ → /max kide/   'he sat until'   52-2, 3

$\|$ahį nąki ka$\|$ → /ahį nax ką/   'when she sat crying'   67-15

6.   Verbs whose stems end in -ti or -hi   optionally undergo the following change when followed by the negative mode marker   ni.

i   → ∅

$\left. \begin{array}{c} t \\ h \end{array} \right\} → x$

$\|$kohi + ni$\|$ → /kox ni/   'they were unwilling'   28-7

$\|$nk + duti + ni$\|$ → $\|$nduti + ni$\|$ (16)

→ /ndux ni/   'I do not eat'   91-138

$\|$nk + dǫhi + ni$\|$ → $\|$ndǫhi + ni$\|$ (16)

→ /ndox ni/   'I do not see'   109-30

$\|$ku + cuti + ni$\|$ → /kucux ni/   'he was not red'   114-40

$\|$ku + ay + yuhi + ni$\|$ → $\|$kay + yuhi + ni$\|$ (8)

→ $\|$kayuhi + ni$\|$ (10)

→ /kayux ni/   'you do not think'   160-11

But:

$\|$duti + ni$\|$ → /duti ni/   'he did not eat it'   144-12

Stems ending in -si optionally undergo only the first step in this rule:

$$i \to \emptyset / \underline{\quad} ni$$

$$\| nk + \emptyset + kidusi + ni \| \to \| axkidusi + ni \| \quad (23)$$

$$\to /axkidus\ ni/ \quad \text{'I did not take it from him'}$$

141-27

But:

$$\| ku + si + ni \| \to /kusi\ ni/ \quad \text{'he did not step in it'} \quad 71-2$$

7. The dative marker ki (see 743.2) is subject to the following rule:

$$\| ki \| \to /kiy/ \ / \underline{\quad} V$$

$$\| ki + E + tu \| \to /kiyetu/ \quad \text{'they said to him'} \quad 37-7$$

$$\| ay + nk + ki + oxpa \| \to \| ay + nk + kiyoxpa \|$$

$$\to \| ya̧k + kiyoxpa \| \quad (24)$$

$$\to /ya̧kiyoxpa/ \quad (10)$$

'(they) drank it for me'   69-4

$$\| ay + nk + ki + o + tu + te \| \to \| ay + nk + kiyotu\ te \|$$

$$\to \| ya̧k + kiyotu\ te \| \quad (24)$$

$$\to /ya̧xkiyotu\ te/ \quad (5)$$

'shoot at it for me!'   85-3

There is one counter-example to this rule; I suspect a glottal stop was inserted before the root:

$$\| ki + i̧ \| \to /kii̧/ \quad \text{'they were drinking it for him'} \quad 69-2$$

8. $V_1 V_1 \rightarrow V_1$

$V_1 V_2 \rightarrow V_2$

This rule is optional with compounds and across word boundaries, and mandatory otherwise.

Examples:

$\|$ ku + ay + o̧ni ni $\|$ → /kayo̧ ni/   'you do not make it'

38-4 (cf. also rule 9)

$\|$ ku + uwe ni $\|$ → /kuwe ni/   'he could not get into...'

24-16

$\|$ so̧pxi + o̧ni $\|$ → /so̧pxo̧ni/   'it makes flour'   (=wheat)

257b

$\|$ ohi so̧sa + axehe $\|$ → /ohi so̧saxehe/   'one sitting on ten'

(=11)   240a

$\|$ ohi dani + axehe $\|$ → /ohi danaxehe/   'three sitting on ten'

(=13)   240a

$\|$ tạto̧ + ahi $\|$ → /tạtahi/   'panther skin'   272b

8.1   There are a few words where two vowels are adjacent to each other in apparent contradiction to this rule. I have no explanation for them, except that since they are all short words, dropping one of the vowels might have led to unwanted ambiguities.

     nao̧   'day'

     yao̧   'sing'

     hauti   'be sick'

     ndao   'here'

9.   With the exception of reduplicated stems and the reciprocal kiki (see 743.3), two morphophonemically identical syllables can never be adjacent to each other.   It appears that it is the first morpheme which is dropped, since less vital information is lost this way:

$\parallel$ noxe yukedi dixya̦ $\parallel$ → /noxe yuke dixya̦/

'whenever they chase them'   17-31

$\parallel$ ku + ku ni $\parallel$ → /ku ni/ 'she does not give'   43-6

$\parallel$ tehi + yE + ni + ni $\parallel$ → /tehiya ni/   'you must not kill him'

(fem.)   155-31

$\parallel$ ku + atamini ni $\parallel$ → $\parallel$ katamini ni $\parallel$ (8)

→ /katami ni/ 'he never works'   166-20

One counter-example needs to be noted:

$\parallel$ kite + te $\parallel$ → /kite te/   'she wanted to hit him'   94-200

10. $\parallel C_1 C_1 \parallel$ → $/C_1/$

$\parallel$ ku + pani ha + ay + YE $\parallel$ → $\parallel$ kupani hay + YE $\parallel$ (8)

→ /kupani haye/   'did you lose it? '   132-20

$\parallel$ ca ha + ay + YE $\parallel$ → $\parallel$ ca hay + YE $\parallel$ (8)

→ /ca haye/   'you kill'   141-4

$\parallel$ ay + nk + kiputka $\parallel$ → $\parallel$ ya̦k + kiputka $\parallel$ (24)

→ /ya̦kiputka/   'you are sitting by me'

143-6

$\|$ ku + ay + yuhi ni $\|$ → $\|$ kay + yuhi ni $\|$ (8)

→ $\|$ kay + yux ni $\|$ (2)

→ /kayux ni/   'you do not think'   160-11

11.   XV#CY → XCY

This optional rule deals with final vowel deletion in compounds.

$\|$ ina + toho $\|$ → $\|$ intoho $\|$ → /įtoho/   (12)

'sun + falls' = 'sunset'   52-2

$\|$ kąxi + koniška $\|$ → /kąxkoniška/   'bee + bottle' =

'hornet's nest'   206a

$\|$ cake + pocka $\|$ → /cakpocka/   'hand + round' = 'fist'   260b

Rule 10 often leads to some unexpected clusters:

a.   geminates:

$\|$ ąsepi + poxka $\|$ → / ąseppoxka/   'axe + round' =

'sledge hammer'   93-193

$\|$ ayapi + pa + są $\|$ → /ayappasą/   'eagle + head + white' =

'bald eagle'   88-78

b.   others:

$\|$ ndesi + xidi $\|$ → /ndesxidi/   'snake + chief' = 'rattlesnake'

86-23

$\|$ tohoxka + waxi $\|$ → /tohoxkwaxi/   'horse + shoe' =

'horseshoe'   121-2

$\|$cake + ptaxe$\|$ → /cakptaxe/   'hand + flat' =

'palm of the hand'   260b

$\|$ti + itka + sa̧hi̧$\|$ → /titksa̧hi̧/   'house + in + other side (?)'

= 'ceiling'   276b

12.   Vn#C → Ṿ̧C

This rule deals with the nasalization of vowels in morpheme final position and the subsequent loss of /n/. It applies to compounds.

$\|$ina + toho$\|$ → $\|$in + toho$\|$ (11)   → /i̧toho/   'sunset'

52-2

$\|$dani + hudi$\|$ → $\|$dan + hudi$\|$ (11)   → /da̧hudi/   'eight'

180b

The following rules deal with person markers for both nouns and verbs. (For their discussion, see 610 and 630.)

13.   All stems beginning with /h/ and certain stems beginning with /y/ (morphophonemically represented by $\|$Y$\|$) are subject to the following rule. It is mandatory for stems beginning with /h/, and optional for those beginning with /y/.

$$\text{stem semi-vowel} \rightarrow \emptyset \Big/ \begin{array}{l} \|nk\|\_\_\_ \\ \|ay\|\_\_\_ \end{array}$$

Examples:

$\|$ nk + Yeh̥o + ni $\|$ → /nkehǫni/   'I know'   117-6-11

$\|$ nk + hauti + xti $\|$ → /nkauti xti/   'I am very ill'   143-11

$\|$ nk + Yihi $\|$ → /nkihi/   'I think'   143-20-33

$\|$ kuhi + yą̣k + YE + te $\|$ → /kuhi yą̣ke te/

'he wishes to raise me'   156-5

$\|$ nk + hamaki $\|$ → /nkamaki/   'we are (standing)'   164-8

$\|$ nk + hu + di $\|$ → /nkudi/   'I come from'   198b

$\|$ ay + hamaki $\|$ → /ayamaki/   'you pl. are (sitting)'   133-23

$\|$ ay + hauti $\|$ → /ayauti/   'you are sick'   195b

$\|$ ay + Yeh̥o + ni $\|$ → /ayehǫni/   'you know'   291a

(see also rule 10)

$\|$ ay + Yihi $\|$ → /ayihi/   'you think'   292a   (see also rule 10)

It should be stressed that not all roots beginning with /y/ are
subject to this rule. Only those undergoing the change are marked
by a capital.

Counter-examples:

$\|$ nk + yaǫni $\|$ → /nkyaǫni/   'I sing'   166-17

$\|$ nk + yą̣ni $\|$ → /nkyą̣ni/   'I sleep'   290b

The first person morpheme <u>nk</u> is subject to the following
rules:

14. $\|$ nk $\|$ → /x/ /___k.   This rule applies before roots as well
as before the dative marker /ki/.

$\|$ nk + ku $\|$ → /xku/   'I come back hither'   113-23

$\|$ nk + kidi $\|$ → /xkidi/   'I come home'   75-60

$\|$ nk + kaha $\|$ → /xkaha/   'I mean'   156-15

$\|$ nk + kici $\|$ → /xkici/   'I am unwilling'   159-5

$\|$ nk + kite $\|$ → /xkite/   'I shoot at'   55-22

$\|$ nk + ku $\|$ → /xku/   'I give'   75-66

and:

$\|$ nk + ki + yoha̧ + ni $\|$ → /xkiyoha̧ ni/   'I wish for him... not'

165-10

$\|$ nk + ki + ku $\|$ → /xkiku/   'I gave him'   147-32

$\|$ nk + ∅ + ki + E + di $\|$ → /axkiyedi/   'I told him'   144-23

15. $\|$ nk $\|$ → /o̧/ /___n, and optionally before /m/ and /p/.

$\|$ nk + na̧ki $\|$ → /o̧na̧ki/   'I sit'   109-37

$\|$ nk + ne + ni $\|$ → /o̧ne ni/   'I do not stand'   164-14

$\|$ nk + naxe $\|$ → /o̧naxe/   'I hear'   231b

$\|$ nk + nayetu $\|$ → /o̧nayetu/   'we swallow'   233b

$\|$ nk + ni $\|$ → /o̧ni/   'I walk'   236a

$\|$ nk + misitu $\|$ → /o̧misitu/   'we sneeze'   230b

$\|$ nk + mixkite + di $\|$ → /o̧mixktedi/   'I perspire'

4800:342:17

$\|$ nk + pxitu $\|$ → /o̧pxitu /   'we cheat'   246a

$\|$ nk + pxatu $\|$ → /o̧pxatu/   'we swim'   246a

<u>But:</u>

‖ nk + pastuki ‖ → /nkpastuki/   'I sew'   142-5

16.   ‖ nk ‖ → /n/ /___other consonants

‖ nk + ya̧ ni ‖ → /nya̧ ni/   'I hate him'   19-11

‖ nk + tE + hi ‖ → ‖ nk ta hi ‖   (1)

→ /nta hi/   'I shall die'   61-18

‖ nk + de ‖ → /nde/   'I go'   147-32

‖ nk + duti + tu ‖ → ‖ nk + duxtu ‖   (2)

→ /nduxtu/   'we ate'   162-23

‖ nk + cude ‖ → /ncude/   'I empty'   166-31

‖ nk + mixyi ‖ → /nmixyi/   'I move in a circle'   230a

‖ nk + sihu + tu ‖ → /nsihutu/   'we are barefooted'   254b

The following examples show that this rule is optional before all consonants except /d/ (for which it is mandatory), and /m/ which will either require rule 15 or 16.

‖ nk + si̧to ‖ → /nksi̧to/   'I am a boy'   129-5

‖ nk + Yeho̧ ‖ → /nkyeho̧/   'I know'   149-15

‖ nk + tE ni ‖ → /nkta ni/   (1)   'I (will) not die'   162-25

‖ nk + cu ‖ → /nkcu/   'I planted'   266b

17.   ‖ nk ‖ → /nk/ /___V

‖ nk + o̧ ‖ → /nko̧/   'I make'   127-11

‖ nk + a̧xti ‖ → /nka̧xti/   'I am a woman'   128-20

‖ nk + i̧spe ‖ → /nki̧spe/   'I know how'   138-17

‖ nk + atamini ‖ → /nkatamini/   'I work'   146-2

‖ nk + į ‖ → /nkį/   'I drink'   158-9

‖ nk + umą ‖ → /nkumą/   '(we) bathe'   283b

The second person morpheme ‖ ay ‖ is subject to the following rules:

18.   (opt.) ‖ ay ‖ → /aya ~ ya/ /___k, x

‖ ay ‖ → /ya/:

‖ ay + kide ‖ → /yakide/   'you go home'   161-13

‖ ay + ki ‖ → /yaki/   'you carry on your back'   161-17

‖ ku + ay + ki + yohą + ni ‖ → /kuyakiyohą ni/

'she does not wish for him...'   165-9

‖ ay + ku ‖ → /yaku/   'you come back'   166-9

‖ ay ‖ → /aya/:

‖ ay + kitupe ‖ → /ayakitupe/   'you carry on your shoulder'

150-26

‖ ay + kihǫ ‖ → /ayakihǫ/   'you have brought it back'   153-15

19.   ‖ ay ‖ → /i/ /___C

‖ ay + duti + tu ‖ → ‖ ay + duxtu ‖   (2)

→ /iduxtu/   'you pl. eat'   31-4

‖ ay + dǫhi ‖ → /idǫhi/   'you see'   50-6

‖ ay + dą ‖ → /idą/   'you take'   92-160

‖ ay + sąki ‖ → / isąki/   'you are a girl'   129-14

‖ ay + pastuki ‖ → /ipastuki/   'you sew'   142-4

∥ay + toho∥ → /itoho/   'you fall'   153-28

∥ay + kaha∥ → /ikaha/   'you mean'   156-13

∥ay + ni + tu∥ → /initu/   'you pl. walk'   161-11

∥ay + mixyi∥ → /imixyi/   'you move in a circle'   230a

∥ay + yuhi + tu∥ → /iyuxtu/   'you pl. thought'   292a

20.   ∥ay∥ → /ay ~ y ~ iy/ /___V

∥a̲y̲∥ → /a̲y̲/:

∥ay + i̦sihi + xti∥ → /ayi̦sihi xti/   'you fear greatly'   13-17

∥ay + ande∥ → /ayande/   'you are'   57-46

∥ay + ihi̦∥ → /ayihi̦/   'you arrived'   125-13

∥ay + i̦kxihi∥ → /ayi̦kxihi/   'you laugh'   146-18

∥ay + a̦hi̦∥ → /aya̦hi̦/   'you cry'   177a

∥a̲y̲∥ → /y̲/:

∥ay + andE hi ni∥ → /yanda hi ni/   'you shall be so'

56-42/3

∥ay + o∥ → /yo/   'you shoot'   65-4

∥ay + a̦hi̦∥ → /ya̦hi̦/   'you cry'   68-16

∥ay + akanaki∥ → /yakanaki/   'you got out'   85-14

∥ay + i̦spE∥ → /yi̦spe/   'you know how'   138-15

∥a̲y̲∥ → /i̲y̲/:

∥ay + E∥ → /iye/   'you say'   67-13

∥ay + i̦hi̦∥ → /iyi̦hi̦/   'you arrive'   108-20

∥ay + a̦hi̦∥ → /iya̦hi̦/   'you cry'   146-17

Some examples in the data have these allomorphs in free variation:

<u>xaha</u>: 'sit down'

    eke xyi dį yaxaha hi ko   'well, why don't you sit down

                (you have been talking about it so long

                without doing it)?' 160-26

    eke xyi di ixaha hi ko   'well, why don't you sit down

                (you have been talking about it so long

                without doing it)?' 160-27

<u>įhį</u>: 'arrive at a place'

    eyą iyįhį ką   'when you go there' 108-20

    heyą ayįhi ko   'when you arrive there' 92-171

<u>ǫ</u>: 'do, make'

    kak ayǫ   'what are you doing?' 68-16

    kawak iyǫ   'what are you doing?' 85-20

<u>E</u>: 'say'

    kawak iye   'what are you saying?' 66-7

    kak aye   'what are you saying?' 67-10

See also ‖ay + ąhį‖ 'you cry' in the immediately preceding group.

Rules 21-24 deal with combinations of personal affixes (e. g. 'first person acting on second'), and as such refer only to verbs.

      <u>1st person acting on 2nd:</u>   ‖nk + ay‖

21. $\|\,nk + ay\,\| \rightarrow /\underset{\zeta}{i}/\ /\_\_\_C$

   $\|\,nk + ay + naxtE\,\| \rightarrow /\underset{\zeta}{i}naxte/$ 'I kick you'   13-12

   $\|\,nk + ay + n\underset{\zeta}{o}de\,\| \rightarrow /\underset{\zeta}{i}n\underset{\zeta}{o}de/$ 'I throw you away'   86-33

   $\|\,nk + ay + d\underset{\zeta}{o}hi\,\| \rightarrow /id\underset{\zeta}{o}hi/$ 'I see you'   137-8

   $\|\,nk + ay + ky\underset{\zeta}{a}hi\ daha\ dandE\,\| \rightarrow /\underset{\zeta}{i}ky\underset{\zeta}{a}hi\ daha\ dande/$

                           'I will scold you all'   139-31

   $\|\,nk + ay + kaha\ daha\,\| \rightarrow /\underset{\zeta}{i}kaha\ daha/$ 'I mean you (pl.)'

            156-18

There is one major exception to rule 21:

$\|\,nk + ay + ku\,\|$ does not generate $/\underset{\zeta}{i}ku/$ as expected, but instead gives /nyiku/ 'I give you' (76-86-, 124-24, 129-18, 160-16, etc.).

22. $\|\,nk + ay\,\| \rightarrow /ny/\ /\_\_\_V$

   $\|\,nk + ay + \underset{\zeta}{i}dahi\,\| \rightarrow /ny\underset{\zeta}{i}dahi/$ 'I seek you'   17-29 (note)

   $\|\,nk + ay + E\ di\,\| \rightarrow /nye\ di/$ 'I say to you'   145-27

   $\|\,nk + ay + akuwE\ dande\,\| \rightarrow \|\,nk + ay + akuwa\ dande\,\|$ (1)

                     $\rightarrow$ /nyakuwa dande/   'I will take you along'

            150-33

   $\|\,heti\ nk + ay + \underset{\zeta}{o}\,\| \rightarrow /heti\ ny\underset{\zeta}{o}/$ 'I am doing so to you'

            154-27

23. **1st person on 3rd:** $\|\,nk + \emptyset\,\| \rightarrow \|\,nk\,\|$ Subject to rules 13-17 with the following addition:

$\| nk + \emptyset \| \rightarrow /ax/ /\underline{\quad} k$

$\| nk + \emptyset + kte \| \rightarrow /axkte/$ 'I hit him'   140-21

$\| nk + \emptyset + kte + tu \| \rightarrow /axktetu/$ 'we hit him'   140-26

$\| nk + \emptyset + ki + e\ di \| \rightarrow \| nk + \emptyset + kiye\ di \|$ (7)

$\rightarrow /axkiye\ di/$ 'I told her'   143-17

$\| nk + \emptyset + ki + ku \| \rightarrow /axkiku/$ 'I got it for him'   147-32

24.   <u>2nd person on 1st</u>: $\| ay + nk \|$

   $\| ay + nk \| \rightarrow /ya̧k/.$ This morpheme is subject to
rules 13-17.

   $\| ay + nk + dusi \| \rightarrow /yandusi/$ 'you take me'   72-8

   $\| cidi + ay + nk + o̧ \| \rightarrow /\ cidi\ yako̧/$

   'you do anything for me'   89-94

$\| ku + ay + nk + Yeho̧\ ni \| \rightarrow /kuya̧kyeho̧\ ni/$

   'don't you know me?'   122-9

$\| ay + nk + ku \| \rightarrow /yaxku/$ 'you give to me'   129-19

$\| ay + nk + i̧cpe \|$ $/ya̧ki̧cpe/$ 'you laughed at me'   162-5

$\| ay + nk + ipudahi \| \rightarrow /ya̧ki̧pudahi/$ 'you protect me'

   147-13

25.   The subjunctive mode marker $\| xo \|$ (see 635) is subject
to the following rule:

$$\| xo \| \rightarrow /xyo/\ \genfrac{}{}{0pt}{}{i\underline{\quad}}{i̧\underline{\quad}}$$

Examples:

‖ o̧ nani xo ‖ → /o̧ nani <u>xyo</u>/   'she must have done it'   44-6/7

‖ ande xa xti x o ‖ → /ande xya xti <u>xyo</u>/   'he shall always live,

provided...'   158-11   (see also rule 26)

‖ nk + ay + kte xo ‖ → /i̧kte <u>xo</u>/   'I will hit you if'

13-11   (see also rule 21)

‖ nk + te so̧sa xo ‖ → /nkte so̧sa <u>xo</u>/   'I will die once'   62-20

26.   The habitual   mode marker   ‖ xa ‖   (see 635) is subject
to the following optional rule:

$$\| xa \| \rightarrow /xya/ \ /V^f \_\_\_$$

‖ ande xa ‖ → /ande xya/   'she is always so'   109-41

‖ supi na̧ki xa ‖ → / supi na̧ki xya/   'he usually has a black

spot (sitting)'   111-3

‖ ku + cuti ni xa ‖ → /kucux ni xya/   'it is not usually red'

114-40   (see also rule 6)

‖ catu + xa ‖ → / catu xa/   'they die regularly'   38-5

‖ oyihi xti tu xa ‖ → /oyihi xti tu xa/   'they always want it

badly'   88-79

The following examples show that this rule is optional:

‖ kasa̧tu ni xa ‖ → /kasa̧tu ni xa/   'they are not usually

white'   31-13

‖ ahi̧sketa̧ yuke xa ‖ → /ahi̧sketa̧ yuke xa/   'they are

usually covetous'   52-18

‖nkaduti te xa‖ → /nkaduti te xa/   'I am still hungry'

133-7

27.   The auxiliary <u>ande</u> (see 941.1) is subject to the following

rule:

$$\begin{array}{l} \|e\| \to \emptyset \\ \|d\| \to t \end{array} \Big/ \underline{\quad} k$$

‖nkande + kaca‖ → /nkant kaca/   'I was, but'   75-67

‖hande + kide‖ → /hant kide/   'she was, until'   89-108

‖hande + kike‖ → /hant kike/   'he was, though'   90-119

CHAPTER II

MORPHOLOGY

500. Introduction

There are three word classes in Biloxi: verbs, substantives (nouns and pronouns), and particles. The first two classes are identifiable in that they are formed by the juxtaposition of a stem plus affixes. Particles, on the other hand, are negatively defined as elements to which inflectional affixes cannot be added.

Verbs can be defined morphologically since they are characterized by the numerous affixes which may accompany them. In addition to the person and number markers which are always present, verbs may also be marked as dative, reciprocal, reflexive, and/or instrumental constructions. They may also be marked by the presence of mode markers, the object specifier, and auxiliaries. Syntactically, they are the last or the next-to-last element within a clause.

Verbs are inflected for person, number, and mode. There are three persons (1st, 2nd, and 3rd) and two numbers (singular and plural). Although Dorsey occasionally glosses forms as 'dual', there is no solid evidence in the corpus of a dual form in

Biloxi. There are numerous mode markers, some of which are
very easy to define, others whose meaning remains elusive.

The basic order of morphemes within a verb is as follows:

(ku) (see 635.8)	person prefixes	thematic prefixes	dative reciprocal, reflexive prefixes	instru- mentals
		root	number suffixes	mode markers

The tense of a verb may be indicated either through a mode
marker or an auxiliary, but it is not a necessary part of any
verbal construction. Thus de can mean either 'he is going' or 'he
went'. To be more specific one can say de ande, 'he is going' or
da ǫ, 'he went'.

Verbs are divided into two groups: classificatory verbs and
normal verbs. The classificatory verbs serve an almost auxiliary
function to normal verbs, and specify the axis of the subject:
standing, sitting, reclining, etc. All three persons are inflected
for number in classificatory verbs, but curiously, only the second
and third persons are inflected for person.

Normal verbs, meaning all others, can have either an active
or a stative meaning. There are no morphological grounds for
separating active and stative verbs, but there is a syntactic
idiosyncrasy that points to the probability that they were once two

different categories, viz. ko is the nominal particle used when the
main verb of the sentence is stative (see 934):

aya̧ si̧hi ne ko te di   'the standing tree is dead'   118-5

ayewi ko udunahi   'he faces the door'   136-20

cf. ayewi (∅) uwe dedi   'he entered at the door'   138-21.

Nouns are more difficult to define than verbs, since there
are no nominal affixes which cannot also be verbal affixes. We
thus have to define them negatively as those inflectable elements
which cannot be marked as dative, reciprocal, reflexive and/or
instrumental. In addition, they are not marked by mode markers
or auxiliaries. Syntactically, they usually appear as the first or
second element of a sentence.

Nouns are divided into two groups: those which are
inflected, and others--the large majority--which are not. The
first group is inflected for person and number; nominal person and
number markers are identical to verbal ones.

Nouns can be derived from verbs, or from the juxtaposition
of a noun $+\begin{Bmatrix}\text{noun}\\\text{verb}\end{Bmatrix}$ stem.

Personal pronouns are based on the root indi, and are
inflected for person and number. There is evidence that the
demonstrative pronouns he and de were once inflected for number,
although since the plural forms are found very rarely in the
corpus, it is probable that they were obsolescent when Dorsey
was collecting his data.

Particles are extremely numerous and serve varied
syntactic functions: noun phrase markers, connectives, interjections, adverbials, etc. Some adverbials are derived and are
discussed in the second half of this chapter. Other particles will
be discussed at greater length under syntax.

The following working definitions may be helpful for the
discussion of morphology:

root:	a monomorphemic base.
stem:	anything that can occur with inflectional affixes. It may be simply a root, or it may be a root with several derivational affixes.
affix:	a bound morpheme; may be ∅.
construction:	forms containing at least one root and one affix.
kernel verb:	a verbal stem + person and number markers.
non-kernel affix:	all verbal affixes except person and number markers.

600. Inflection

610. Nouns

Biloxi nouns are divided into two classes: those which are
inflected for possession and those which are not. The first class

is composed of body parts and kin terms which are obligatorily inflected, and a few intimate personal possessions which are optionally inflected. All other nouns are uninflected.

The person markers for inflected nouns are as follows:

nk-   1st person

ay-   2nd person

∅-   3rd person

-tu pluralizes the personal prefix. The number of the noun is expressed only syntactically.

For the morphophonemic rules regarding person and number markers, see rules 2, 3, 13-20.

611.   Examples of inflected nouns follow.

611.1   Body parts

dodi   'throat'

    ndodi   'my throat'   133-9-11

    idodi   'your throat'   133-15

    dodi   'his, her throat'   133-17

    ndoxtu   'our throat'   133-12-14

    idoxtu   'your (pl) throats'   133-16

    doxtu   'their throats'   133-18

cake   'hand'

    nkcake   'my hand'   153-24

    icake   'your hand'   153-25

    cake   'his hand'   260b

    nkcaktu   'our hands'   260b

    icaktu   'your (pl.) hands'   260b

    caktu   'their hands'   149-22

ihi   'mouth'[1]

    nkihi   'my mouth'   199b

    yihi   'your mouth'   138-23

    ihi   'his mouth'   138-24

    nkihitu   'our mouths'   199b

    yihitu   'your (pl.) mouths'   199b

    ihitu   'their mouths'   199b

isu   'teeth'

    nkisu   'my teeth'   140-17

    ayisu   'your teeth'   140-16

    isu   'his teeth'   140-18

    nkisutu   'our teeth'   203a

    ayisutu   'your (pl.) teeth'   203a

    isutu   'their teeth'   203a

---

[1]This root is an exception to morphophonemic rule 2.

sponi   'ankle'

    nksponi   'my ankle'   96-247

    isponi   'your ankle'   254b

    sponi   'his, her ankle'   254b

    nksponitu   'our ankles'   254b

    isponitu   'your (pl.) ankles'   254b

    sponitu   'their ankles'   254b

yatka   'jaw'

    nyatka   'my jaw'   289a

    iyatka   'your jaw'   289a

    yatka   'his, her jaw'   289a

    nyatkatu   'our jaws'   289a

    iyatkatu   'your jaws'   289a

    yatkatu   'their jaws'   289a

The following is a complete list of the names of body parts that Dorsey collected; for further reference, see 4800:348, p. 78 ff.

adǫhi̧	'face'	asą̧hi̧ kaskani	'left arm'
ahi	'skin'	asǫti	'shoulder blade'
ahudi ~ ahodi	'bone'	axe	'shoulder'
amanki	'chest of man or woman'	ayixi	'stomach'
		ayitpahi̧	'soft part of abdomen'
anahi̧	'hair'	cake	'hand'
asa̧hi̧	'arm'	cakahi	'fingernail'
asą̧hi̧ spewa	'right arm'	cakponi	'wrist'

cakptaxe   'palm of hand'

cakeyati   'middle of palm'

   (='heart of palm')

caktapi   'back of hand'

cakowusi   'fingers'

cakxohi   'thumb' (='old hand')

cakamihi   '1st finger'

caknantenedi   '2nd finger'

cakayika ikcahi   '3rd finger'

   (='next to 4th finger')

cakayika   '4th finger'

cakahudi   'space between

   knuckles'

cindaho   'hip bone'

cindi   'hips'

cinaki   'knee'

cinanta waxehe   'kneepan'

ciwi   'intestines'

cipo   'navel'

coditi   'penis'

daswa   'back'

docaxka   'tonsils'

dodi   'throat'

dokoxe   'hard palate'

doti   'neck' (dodi??)

doxtatka   'adam's apple'

hadixi   'urine'

hai ~ haidi   'blood'

haidixci   'bladder'

haiti   'artery, vein'

   (='blood house')

haikinedi   'spleen'

ihi   'mouth'

ihi yapi   'lips'

ihi yapi tawi   'upper lip'

ihi yapi xwuhi   'lower lip'

isi   'foot'

isi ahi   'toenail'

isi axohi   'big toe'

isi ikcahi axohi   '2nd toe'

isi nantenedi   '3rd toe'

isi ayika ikcahi   '4th toe'

isi ayika   '5th toe'

isi mayini   'sole of foot'

ite   'face, forehead'

icipo   'gall'

ika   'muscle'

istodi   'elbow'

i̧su   'teeth'

kipate   'knuckles'

nato̧   'brain'

naxko   'sideburns'

nindi   'rump'

nixta   'breath'

nixuxwi   'ear'

nixuxwi ahudi   'upper part
    of earlobe'

nixuxwi siopi   'earwax'

nixuxwi tpa̧hi̧   'soft part
    of earlobe'

nixuxwokpe   'perforation
    in ear'

nixuxtitpe   'external opening
    of ear'

pa   'head'

pa aho   'skull'

pa tawi   'crown of head'

pa̧hi̧ o̧ni   'beard'

pa̧hi̧ tawi   'mustache'

pco̧   'nose'

pco̧ ahudi tpa̧hi̧   'septum
    of nose'

pco̧ ahudi tpa̧hi̧ okpe
    'perforation of septum
    of nose'

pco̧ putsi   'ridge of nose'

pco̧tpe   'nostril'

pi   'liver'

pkanaxexe   'lock of hair'

sponi   'ankle'

sponi ahudi   'ankle bone'

spudaxi   'instep'

stuti   'heel of foot'

tacke   'saliva'

taki   'thigh'

tasi   'female breasts'

tasi pudi   'nipples'

taxpadi   'temples'

taxoxka   'rib'

tayo   'cheek'

ta̧ihudi   'spine'

te uso   'eyebrows'

tiamḩi   'eyelashes'

ti̧ska   'windpipe, back of neck'

tuco̧   'eyes'

tuco̧ ahi tawi   'upper eyelid'

tuco̧ ahi xwuhi

    'lower eyelid'

tuco̧ sa̧   'cornea'

    (='eye, white')

tuco̧ supka   'iris'

    (='eye, blackish')

tuco̧ susupi   'pupil'

    (='eye, very black')

tuksi   'armpits'

yakhu   'lung'

yanti   'heart'

ya̧ska   'kidney'

yatka pso̧ti   'chin'

    (='sharp jaw')

yatki̧sudi   'molars'

    (='jaw teeth')

yeci   'tongue'

yisiki   'vulva'

yo   'body'

yonixtadi   'pulse'

    ('body's breath')

yukpe   'leg'

yukpe putsi   'tibia'

yukpe i̧ti   'calf'

isi wusi   'toes'

611.2   Kin terms

    adi   'father'

        nkadi   'my father'   130-10, 11

        iyadi   'your father'   158-18

        adi   'his father'   113-33

        nkaxtu   'our father'   113-16

        axtu   'their father'   112-11, 113-32

yįkati   'husband'

    nyįkati   'my husband'   4800:345-6

    iyįkati   'your husband'   293b

    yįkati   'her husband'   38-9

kąxo   'grandfather'

    xkąxo   'my grandfather'   4800:345-1

    kąxo   'his grandfather'   75-78

yįki   'son'

    nyįki   'my son'   4800:345-2

    iyįki   'your son'   294a

    yįki   'his son'   149-17

yįkadodi   'grandson'

    nyįkadodi   'my grandson'   20-25

    iyįkadodi   'your grandson'   294a

    yįkadodi   'his grandson'   294a

tando   'younger brother'   (female speaker)

    nktando   'my younger brother'   269b

    itando   'your younger brother'   269b

    tando   'her younger brother'   38-8

    nktandotu   'our younger brother'   269b

    itandotu   'your (pl.) younger brother'   269b

    tandotu   'their younger brother'   269b

sǫtkaka   'younger brother'   (male speaker)

    nksǫtkaka   'my younger brother'   257b

    isǫtkaka   'your younger brother'   257b

    sǫtkaka   'his younger brother'   130-15

    nksǫtkakatu   'our younger brother'   257b

    isǫtkakatu   'your (pl.) younger brother'   257b

    sǫtkakatu   'their younger brother'   257b

kǫni ~ ǫni   'mother'

    nkǫni   'my mother'   4800:345-1

    ayǫni   'your mother'   130-12, 13

    kǫni   'his mother'   93-179

    ǫni   'his, her mother'   284b

yįkǫni   'wife'   (='little mother')

    nyįkǫni   'my wife'   4800:345-6

    yįkǫ   'his wife'   85-2

kǫkǫ   'grandmother'

    xkokǫ   'my grandmother'   **4800:345-1**

    ikǫkǫ   'your grandmother'   217b

    kǫkǫ   'his grandmother'   19-16

yǫki   'daughter'

    nkiyǫki   'my daughter'   159-5

    nyǫki   'my daughter'   4800:345-2

    iyǫki   'your daughter'   296a

    yǫki   'his or her daughter'   296a

yǫkadodi   'granddaughter'   (son's daughter')

    nyǫkadodi   'my granddaughter'   4800:345-2

    iyǫkadodi   'your granddaughter'   296b

    yǫkadodi   'his or her son's daughter'   296b

taki   'elder sister'   (male speaker)

    ntaki   'my elder sister'   4800:345-4

    yataki   'your elder sister'   272a

    taki   'his sister'   50-7

taska   'younger sister'   (female speaker)

    nktaska   'my younger sister'   272a,   4800:345-5

    yitaska   'your younger sister'   272a

    taska   'her younger sister'   130-14

The following is a list of all the kin terms that Dorsey collected.
The glosses given are the basic ones: for further semantic
information on them, readers are advised to check 4800:345.

adi   'father'

acki   'his or her father's younger brother'

aduwo   'his or her father's elder brother'

ckani   'sister-in-law'

ini   'his elder brother'

inoni   'her elder sister'

kaxo   'grandfather'

kaxo akitkoxi   'great grandfather'

kaxo kitko akitkoxi   'great great grandfather'

k̨axo kitko kitko akitkoxi   'great great great grandfather'

kǫkǫ   'grandmother, mother-in-law'

kǫkǫ akitkoxi   'great grandmother'

kǫkǫ kitko akitkoxi   'great great grandmother'

kǫkǫ kitko kitko akitkoxi   'great great great grandmother'

kyako yįki   'son's son's son'

kyako akitkoxi yįki   'son's son's son's son'

kyako yįkakitkoxi   'daughter's daughter's son's son'

kyako yǫki   'son's son's daughter'

kyako akitkoxi yǫki   'son's son's son's daughter'

kyako yǫkakitkoxi   'daughter's daughter's son's daughter'

ǫni ~ kǫni   'mother'

ǫni uwo   'mother's elder sister'

sǫtkaka   'his younger brother'

tahani   'wife's brother'

tando ~ tando aka   'her younger brother'

tando noxti   'her elder brother'

takaka   'his younger sister'

taki ~ takxohi   'his elder sister'

taska   'her younger sister'

tohǫni   'daughter-in-law'

tohǫnoxti   'father-in-law'

tondi   'son-in-law'

tǫni   'his or her father's elder sister'

toni aka   'his or her father's younger sister'

tukani   'mother's brother'

tukaninoxti   'his or her mother's elder brother'

tukani aka   'his or her mother's younger brother'

tuksiki   'elder sister's son'

tuksiki aka   'younger sister's son'

tusoki   'elder sister's daughter'

tusoki aka   'younger sister's daughter'

yiki   'his or her son'

yikadodi   'his or her son's son'

yikakitkoxi   'daughter's son's son'

yikati   'husband

yikoni   'wife'

yikayiki   'husband's brother' (='potential husband')

yoki   'daughter'

yokadodi   'son's daughter'

yokado yiki   'son's daughter's son'

yokado yoki   'son's daughter's daughter'

yokayiki   'daughter's son'

yokayoki   'daughter's daughter'

yokakitkoxi   'daughter's son's daughter'

611.3   Intimate personal possessions. This group is only optionally inflected.

ti ~ ati   'house'

    nkti   'my house'   22-5

    nkati   'my house'   275a

    iti   'your house'   73-17

    ayati   'your house'   275a

    ati   'his house'   275a

    nkatitu   'our house'   275a

    ayatitu (?)   'your (pl.) house'   275a

    atitu (?)   'their house'   275a

doxpe   'shirt'

    idoxpe   'your shirt'   140-33

uduxpe   'clothing'   (generic term)

    nkuduxpe   'my clothing'   138-19

    uduxpe   'his or her clothing'   138-18

manki   'dress'

    imanki   'your dress'   140-32

620. Pronouns

621. Independent personal pronouns.

Non-affixal personal pronouns are always optional, and as
such seem to be used for emphatic purposes only. In the singular,
they can be used either as subjects or objects, while in the plural
they are used only as subjects. [The suffix -daha (see 633.3)

marks plural objects.] These pronouns are based on the root

indi, to which are added the normal person and number markers.

(See 610 above.)

nkindi	'I'	nkįxtu	'we'
ayindi	'you'	ayįxtu	'you all'
indi	'he, she, it'	įxtu	'they'

Morphophonemic rule 3 accounts for the changes in the plural

forms. Singular indi has free variants ind and int before /h/ and

/k/. Likewise, plural įxtu can be shortened to įxt under the same

conditions.

622. Demonstrative pronouns

There are two common demonstrative pronouns in Biloxi;

de, 'this', and he, 'that'. Their plural forms are denani and

henani respectively. Both plural forms are very rare, and it

would seem that they are used only when the plurality is not

obvious from the rest of the phrase. In noun phrases containing

classificatory verbs, for example (see 941.2), plurality is marked

in the verb, and thus the demonstrative is rendered in the

singular:

aya atahi amą de   'these running men'   4800:348; 198+

cǫki xaxaxa amą de   'these standing dogs'   4800:348; 198+

630. Verbs

Biloxi verbs are inflected for person, number, and mode.
The person and number markers are the same as those used in
inflected nouns (see 610):

nk-   1st person

ay-   2nd person

∅-   3rd person

-tu pluralizes the prefix

Verbs with inanimate nouns as subjects are not pluralized.

For the morphophonemic rules regarding verbal person and
number markers, see rules 2, 4, 9, 13-24. Further allomorphy
is described under section 632.

631. Representative examples:

I	<u>nk</u>cudi	'I planted'	22-3, 4
	<u>nk</u>ǫ	'I make (it)'	151-12
you	<u>ya</u>ku	'you are coming back'	92-158
	<u>ay</u>atamini	'you work'	146-1
he,	cacake	'he hung up'	15-3
she	de	'she went'	76-89
we	<u>ndǫxtu</u>	'we see'	184a
	<u>nkįxtu</u>	'we reached'	148-28

you   ay̦o̦tu   'you (pl.) did it'   150-17

   ayakixtu   'have you (pl.) brought it back?'   153-18

they   hetu   'they say it'   156-12

   akuwetu   'they came out in sight'   156-28

632.   In addition, the person markers combine in the following
ways:

<u>1st person on 2nd</u>:   ‖ nk + ay ‖ → /ny ~ i̦/

(see rules 21 and 22)

   i̦kikta dande   'I will hit your...'   125-2

   i̦dunamni   'I bother you'   150-13

   heti <u>nyo̦</u> nyukedi   'we do so to you'   154-28

   <u>ny</u>inkowa   'I depend on you for protection'   155-2

<u>1st person on 3rd</u>:   ‖ nk + ∅ ‖ → ‖ nk ‖ → /nk ~ x ~ n ~ ax/

(see rules 13-17, 23)

   <u>nd</u>o̦xtu   'we saw her'   126-7

   <u>ax</u>kiyedi   'I told her'   143-17

   ca ha<u>x</u>kiya dande   'I will kill him for him'   146-13

   nk<u>i̦</u>cpe   'I laugh at him'   162-3

<u>2nd person on 1st</u>:   ‖ ay + nk ‖ → /ya̦k/

(see rules 13-17, 24)

   etiki <u>ya̦ko̦</u>   'you treated me so'   24-19

   <u>ya̦x</u>kiko̦ daha   'you do it for us'   55-20

   <u>ya̦x</u>kitetu   'you (pl.) hit me'   61-17/18

de hiy ̧ake te   'you wish to send me'   156-8

y ̧axku   'you give it to me'   160-3

2nd person on 3rd: $\|\,\text{ay} + \emptyset\,\| \rightarrow \|\,\text{ay}\,\| \rightarrow$ /i ∼ ay ∼ ya ∼ aya/

          (see rules 18-20)

id ̧ohi   'you see it'   50-6

yakte   'you hit him'   140-22

ay ̧o   'you did it'   150-15

ayakixtu   'have you (pl.) brought it back?'   153-18

ayakuwex   'you (pl.) took him along'   154-33

3rd person on 1st: $\|\,\emptyset + \text{y ̧ak}\,\| \rightarrow$ /y ̧ak/

          (see rules 13-17)

eti y ̧ak ̧oni   'he did thus to me'   33-6

y ̧akyeh ̧o   'he knows me'   122-10

y ̧axkisine   'he stole it from me'   132-2

yad ̧oxpituni   'they do not look at me well'   134-18

3rd person on 2nd: $\|\,\emptyset + \text{ay}\,\| \rightarrow \|\,\text{ay}\,\|$

          (see rules 18-20)

id ̧oxtu   'they see you'   88-75

iyanox tedi   'she wishes to chase you'   93-183

iyetu   'they say to you'   108-16

ikudut ̧atu   'they urged you on'   159-17

<u>3rd person on 3rd</u>: $\| \emptyset + \emptyset \| \to \emptyset$

    ku   'he gave him'   15-9

    hane   'he found him'   26-3

    kiyedi   'he told her'   28-19

    kyąhi   'he scolded him'   33-3

    duti   'he ate it'   85-19

    ca yetu   'they killed them'   141-2

632.1 Ambiguous forms:

    1. The surface manifestations of the 2nd person on 1st forms are the same as the 3rd person on 1st forms. In fact, we have the following identical forms:

        <u>y</u>axtedi   'you hit me, he hit me'   214b

        <u>y</u>ądǫhi   'you see me, he sees me'   184b

    2. In addition, the surface manifestations for 2nd person subj., 2nd person on 3rd, and 3rd person on 2nd, are all identical. We have the following examples:

        <u>i</u>dǫhi   'you see'   (184a)   'you see him'   126-5

                    and 'they see you'   (87-59)

        <u>i</u>yąhį   'you love him, he loves you'   4800:344-1

633. Number markers

633.1 -<u>tu</u> is used to mark animate plural subjects with all verbs except some verbs of motion (see 633.2 below). Representative

examples:

ikcatu ni   'we have not forgotten you'   21-3

nkyehotu ni   'we did not know'   22-8

nkįxtu dande   'we will reach there'   126-2

iksixtu   'you (pl.) are crazy'   93-195

yaktetu   'you (pl.) hit him'   140-25

kiyetu   'they said to him'   37-7

akitatu xa   'they follow it regularly'   38-7

yihixtitu ha ni   'they may have the most'

(fem. sp.)   40-16

-tu is not used in the following three situations:

a. when the auxiliary yuke, 'are', is present, already marking the verb as plural (see 941. 1).

dǫhi yuke   'they were looking at it'   50-12

b. when the plurality of the sentence has been established elsewhere in the sentence:

aditu ką, hidedi nedi   'they climbed up, and were

falling continually'   40-22

(aditu is already plural, and therefore

hidedi need not be).

c. when the immediately following verb is one of motion, and already pluralized:

dą kahi hą   'they took it and were returning'   52-16

(kahi is plural; therefore dą need not be).

Although -tu almost always immediately follows the stem, and is therefore classifiable as a suffix, there is some evidence that it is an enclitic along with the mode markers. Very occasionally, it follows rather than precedes a mode marker:

supi xti tu   'they are very black'   32-16

yihi xti tu ha ni   'they may have the most'   40-16

te ye te tu ką   'when they wished to kill him'   61-17

The examples with xti are not necessarily significant because its position within a verb is freer than that of other modes (see 635:15 below). The third example, however, remains unexplainable.

633.2 Verbs of motion

Some verbs of motion use the prefix a- instead of the suffix -tu to mark plurality. It is inserted immediately before the root. Representative examples:

1. de   'he goes'   181a

    nkade   'we go'   148-28

    ayade   'you (pl.) go'   147-28

    ade   'they go'   148-6

2. kide   'he goes homeward'   182a

    xkade   'we go homeward'   ‖ nk + ki + a + de ‖

    ikade   'you (pl.) go homeward'

    kade   'they go homeward'

3.   hu   'he comes' 149-6

      nka̱hu   'we come' 149-5

      aya̱hu   'you (pl.) come' 149-4

      a̱hu   'they come' 149-3

4.   hi ~ hi̜   'he arrives' 197a

      nka̱hi   'we arrive' 156-30

      aya̱hi   'you (pl.) arrive' 156-29

      a̱hi ~ a̱hi̜   'they arrive' 55-23

      a̱hi te   'come ye!' 56-40

However, other verbs of motion (including some based on these same roots) have -tu as their plural marker:

1.   i̜hi̜   'he arrives' 197a

      nki̜xtu   'we arrive'

      ayi̜xtu   'you (pl.) arrive'

      i̜xtu   'they arrive'

2.   tahi̜   'he runs' 271b

      nkta̱xtu   'we run'

      ita̱xtu   'you (pl.) run'

      ta̱xtu   'they run'

3.   akuwe   'he comes out' 55-14

      nkakuwetu   'we came out in sight' 156-30

      ayakuwetu   'you (pl.) came out in sight' 156-29

      akuwetu   61-15

4. kade 'he goes thither' 182a

   xkad<u>etu</u> 'we go thither'

   ikad<u>etu</u> 'you (pl.) go thither'

   kad<u>etu</u> 'they go thither'

633.3 Plural object marker: <u>daha</u>

<u>daha</u> is used for 1st, 2nd, and 3rd person plural objects.
However, it is necessary only when the plurality of the object has
not already been specified. It follows -<u>tu</u>, and precedes all mode
markers.

Examples:

de yᵉ <u>daha</u> 'he sent them' 52-13

yacǫ <u>daha</u> ǫni 'she named them (in the past)' 57-52

te yᶏka <u>daha</u> 'he killed us' 62-35

yᶏxku <u>daha</u> te 'give it back to us!'

　　　　　　　(female speaker to male addressee) 81-4

ikyᶏhi <u>daha</u> dande 'I will scold you' (pl.) 139-31

nkakixtu <u>daha</u> 'we brought them' 147-29

<u>daha</u> is reduced to <u>ha</u> in two examples:

ikte <u>ha</u> dande 'I will kick you' (pl.) 124-23

nyiku <u>ha</u> dande 'I give it to you' (pl.) 124-25

634. Indefinite object marker: <u>a-</u>

Some verb roots take a prefix <u>a-</u> to indicate an otherwise
unspecified indefinite object.

Examples:

    ki   'carry on the back'

    nka̱ki 'I carried something on my back'   28-12

    da   'gather'

    nka̱da 'I gather things'   40-17

    kikahį 'tell him'

    a̱kikahį   'he told him (the news)'   70-12

    pstuki   'sew'

    a̱pstuki 'sew it'   53-12

    pehe   'pound'

    a̱pehe 'pound something'   75-77

    duti   'eat'

    a̱duti 'eat something'   133-5-8

635. Mode markers

There is a large number of mode markers in Biloxi. Some are extremely common, and present no problems of analysis. Others, instead, appear so rarely that it is difficult to determine their semantic force. The following is a fairly exhaustive list of Biloxi modes, beginning with those most frequently used.

    1. The declarative mode: na, male speaker

                       ni, female speaker

            This is always the last morpheme of any given verbal construction.

na:

nka dande na   'I will say it'   47-22

hetinyǫ nyukedi na   'we are just going to do so to

you'   55-7

nkudi na   'I have been coming back'   108-17, 21

iyadi ya eti na   'this is your father'   158-18

aya tohi yate yuke na   'Negroes are all about'   162-16

kuti mạkde yate ande na   'God is everywhere'   162-18

ni:

nkaduteda ni   'I have finished eating'   39-10

ịkowa ịdahi otu ni   'they themselves hunt and shoot

it'   55-19

eti ni   'this is it'   73-17/18

cicapi xti ni   'it is too slippery'   73-29

yạsi xti ni   'he smells so bad'   108-4

Declarative sentences need not end in na or ni. Indeed,

there are many unmarked declaratives throughout the corpus:

taneks nkaxti   'I am a Biloxi woman'   129-2

cǫki itak nạki   'your dog sits' (= 'you have a dog')

131-3

nkapstuki nkịspe   'I know how to sew'   138-17

2. The interrogative mode: wo, male speaker

∅ , female speaker

This morpheme also appears as the last one in any given verbal construction. It never appears with the declarative mode. There may have been an intonational clue to distinguish otherwise unmarked interrogative sentences from unmarked declarative ones, but it is impossible to determine this from the data.

wo:

etikịnyọni wo   'did I do that to you?'   16-15

iyixọ wo   'have you enough?'   24-9

kawak iye yande wo   'what are you saying?'   61-7

ayạ ade wo   'does the wood burn?'   138-5

cidike ayaọ hi inaki wo   'why do you sit there

singing?'   146-19

iyakakaha daha wo   'do you mean us?'   156-20

∅:

kihaki cidike yukedi   'what kin are they two?'   138-2

ayạ ade   'does the wood burn?'   138-4   (cf. above)

ayakixtu   'have you (pl.) brought it back?'   153-18

kawak e nạki   'what is he saying (as he sits)?'   155-9

ipastuki yande   'were you sewing on it?'   158-22

3. Hortatory mode: hi. This mode marker never appears by itself as part of the principal verb in the sentence. Instead it is almost invariably used in conjunction with the declarative na/ni:

te hiyetu <u>hi</u> na   'you must all kill him'

      62-37 (masc. sp.)

iduti <u>hi</u> na   'you shall eat it'   68-18

inixyi <u>hi</u> na   'he shall play with it roughly'   87-61

nyiku <u>hi</u> na   'I must give it to you'   160-15

nyiku <u>hi</u> ni   'I shall give it to you'   76-86 (fem. sp.)

idǫxtu <u>hi</u> ni   'they shall see you'   88-75

taotu <u>hi</u> ni   'they will shoot deer'   93-182

anda <u>hi</u> ni   'he will be so'   155-25

There is also one example of it with the interrogative <u>wo</u>:

kawa nkǫ ta <u>hi</u> wo   'what will (we) wish to do? '   113-21

When used in an embedded sentence, however, <u>hi</u> need not be accompanied by another mode marker:

ani ndǫ ni nkanda <u>hi</u> yihi   'he thought I should not see

      the water'   33-5/6

yaǫ <u>hi</u> kiyetu   'they told her to sing'   50-15

uto <u>hi</u> kiyedi   'he told him to lie in it'   113-38

4. Potential mode: <u>dande</u>. Follows: <u>tu</u>   precedes: <u>na</u>

                                <u>daha</u>   <u>xe</u>

adutik kikǫ daha <u>dande</u>   'he will make food for

      them'   31-2/3

nka <u>dande</u> na   'I will say it'   47-22

idǫhi <u>dande</u>   'you shall see it'   50-6

ta <u>dande</u>   'he will die'   124-13

ndoxtu uxwi <u>dande</u>   'our throats will be dry'

                ='we will be thirsty'   133-14

įxtu <u>dande</u>   'they will arrive'   135-17

nda <u>dande</u> xye   'I will go (whether he wishes or not)'

        137-22

nyakuwa <u>dande</u>   'I will take you along'   150-33

xohi <u>dande</u>   'it will rain'   151-1

kupi ni xti <u>dande</u>   'there will be very bad weather'

        151-5

5. The optative mode: <u>tE</u> Follows: <u>tu</u>   precedes: <u>dande</u>

                                      <u>daha</u>   ♀

                                                        <u>wo</u>

                                                        <u>hi</u>

                                                        <u>ni</u>

yąxkiyoxpa <u>te</u> yayukedi   'you (pl.) are wishing to drink

        it up for me'   69-5

pis <u>te</u> xti ande   'she strongly desires to suckle'

        74-58

ku <u>te</u> niki   'she does not want to come back'   75-68

kite <u>te</u> hande   'she wanted to hit him'   94-200

ca ye daha <u>te</u>   'he wished to kill them'   112-12

kawa nkǫ <u>ta</u> hi wo   'what will we wish to do?'

        113-21   (see morph. rule 1)

ca hanke te nkamaki na   'we wish to kill them'

    113-22 (masc.)

nkaduti ta dande   'I shall wish to eat'   133-8

    (see morph. rule 1)

nkyehǫ te   'I wish to know'   149-15

ayadutitu te hǫ   'you (pl.) wish to eat'   275b

While te almost always follows the number markers, we do have the following counter-example:

te ye te tu ką   'when they wished to kill him'   61-17

cf.   te hiyetu te ko   'when they wish to kill you'

    95-231

6. The subjunctive mode: xo ~ xyo. Dorsey claims that these two morphs are different (1912:221), but actually their choice depends on morphophonemic rule 25:

$$\|xo\| \rightarrow /xyo/ \Big/ \begin{array}{l} i \underline{\quad\quad} \\[4pt] \underset{\centerdot}{i} \underline{\quad\quad} \end{array}$$

The semantic force of the morpheme is in question, however. The idea of potentiality is involved, as well as contingency. ('I will hit you if,' 'I will come home provided,' etc.). It always appears as the last morpheme within a given verb.

Examples:

kedi xyo   'he must (?) dig it alone'   13-5

inaxta xo   'I will kick you, if'   13-12, 13

nkihį xyo   'I will (?) reach'   19-4

ita <u>xo</u>   'you shall die, if'   70-9

yande xyaxti <u>xyo</u>   'you will always live, if'   70-10

ma są yate yuka <u>xo</u>   'white turkeys will be all about,

provided'   86-37

nde įdǫhi <u>xyo</u>   'I will see you tomorrow (will,

contingency)'   137-8

There are a few examples of <u>xyo</u> appearing with <u>nani</u> which seems
to mean 'can'. Together they take on the meaning of 'must' or
'must have':

ǫ <u>nani</u> <u>xyo</u>   'she must have done it'   44-7

ede te yake daha yandi <u>nani</u> <u>xyo</u>   'this must be the

one who killed us'   61-15/16

ayindi ayǫ <u>nani</u> <u>xyo</u>   'you must have done it'   150-15

įxtu ǫtu <u>nani</u> <u>xyo</u>   'they must have done it'   150-16

ayįxtu ayǫtu <u>nani</u> <u>xyo</u>   'you (pl.) must have done it'

150-17

7. The habitual mode: <u>xa</u> ~ <u>xya</u>   Follows everything but:

<u>na</u>/<u>ni</u>

Dorsey lists two homophonous morphemes here (p. 218), one
being a 'sign of past action', and the other meaning 'customary or
usual action'. I think that there is only one morpheme and that it
denotes customary action.

The choice between the two forms is governed by
morphophonemic rule 26 which is optional:

$$xa \rightarrow xya/V^f\underline{\hspace{1cm}}$$

Examples:

> supixtitu <u>xa</u>   'they are usually very black'   32-17
>
> tiduwi <u>xa</u>   'he alights'   33-12/13
>
> akuwetu <u>xa</u>   'they come out regularly   38-6
>
> akitatu <u>xa</u>   'they follow it'   38-7
>
> awahe yuke <u>xya</u>   'they are crying out as they move'
>
>   38-11
>
> nduti <u>xya</u>   'I usually eat'   55-13
>
> etu <u>xa</u>   'they say always'   96-255, etc.
>
> sindǫ ande <u>xya</u>   'he is always using his tail'   96-16/17
>
> katamini hande <u>xa</u>   'he never works'   166-20
>
> kowohik nǫki <u>xya</u>   'he always sits up above'   111-2

While <u>xa</u> usually appears as the last morpheme of a verb, it can be followed by the declarative marker <u>na</u>/<u>ni</u>:

> nkakiyasi <u>xa</u> <u>na</u>   'I always liked it' (masc.)   16-9/10
>
> nkiyą nkanąpini <u>xa</u> <u>na</u>   'I never sleep until day'
>
>   (masc.)   26-6
>
> nkint ko yinisa ndux ni <u>xa</u> <u>ni</u>   'I never eat buffalo meat'
>
>   (fem.)   55-12
>
> aka ande dedį adute <u>xa</u> <u>ni</u>   'this youngest one is always
>
>   hungry' (fem.)   88-71

etike ko ndux n̓ xa na   'I never eat such (things)'

(masc.)   91-138

kanaxtetu ni xa na   'they never kicked'   128-3

There are various cases where the combination of the habitual and the declarative mode is glossed as 'can':

tǫhį xa na   'he can run' (if he wishes)   218a

akutxyi nkǫ xa na   'I can write'   218a

akutxyi nkukade xa na   'I can read'   218a

eyą nde xa na   'I can go thither' (if I wish)   218a

8. The negative mode: (ku)...ni. It is not clear when ku is necessary, and when ni alone will suffice. We have, for example, de ni, 'he did not go, 144-20, and kude ni, 'it did not go', 28-8; ide ni, 'you did not go', 145-28, and kide ni, 'you did not go', 141-31. ku is never used, however, when the following person marker is nk, 'I'. ku seems to be needed with stems ending in -ni, as well as with the feminine declarative mode marker ni in order to avoid ambiguity. [This is because ‖ni + ni‖ → /ni/ (see morphophonemic rule 9).]

Examples of ku...ni:

kudǫxtu ni xti   'they could not see them at all'   50-14

kute ni   'he did not die'   82-16

kustǫhį ni   'he could not reach it'   89-90

kupi ni xti   'it is so bad' (=not good)   91-140

kunyikte ni 'I do not hit you' 136-19

kuyakiyohą ni 'you do not wish for him' 165-9

Morphophonemic rule 8 accounts for the reduction of /ku/ to /k/ in the following examples:

katoho ni 'not lying down' 52-11

kadǫ ni 'he does not see' (blind) 126-5

kanaxe ni 'she does not hear' (deaf) 126-6

kakititu haye ni (why) 'don't you shut (your mouth)? '
 138-25

kakuduksa hinye ni 'I did not peep at you' 146-16

kapusi ni 'not night' 158-14

kadukce ye ni 'he did not make too much noise'
 165-29

There are various examples in the data of kdux ni, 'he did not eat' (23-7, 15-17, 24-17, 146-10), and none of kudux ni. Since this does not happen to other verbs whose stems begin with /d/, I assume that the reduction has to do with something inherent in the verb duti.

Examples of ni are as follows:

ayį ni dande 'you shall not drink' 13-6

de kox ni 'he did not want to go' 76-79

pice ni ande 'he was not leaping' 82-11

ndux ni xa na 'I do not ever eat it' (masc.) 91-138

duti <u>ni</u>   'he does not eat it'   144-12

ide <u>ni</u>   'you do not go'   145-28

nde <u>ni</u> nkande   'I am not going'   151-9

9. The imperative mode

In his Vice Presidential address to the American Association for the Advancement of Science (1893), Dorsey claims that there are more imperative forms in Biloxi than in other Siouan languages. That may be true, although some of the forms he lists in that address are nowhere to be found in the texts or dictionary. The most common forms found are listed below. It will be noted that when the addressee is plural, the plural marker -<u>tu</u> (or <u>a</u>-) is used. Except for 2nd person negative imperatives, person markers are used only to mark objects.

The formula for the imperative is:

stem + (number marker) + imperative mode marker

All imperative forms but one (see 9.4 below) are marked.

One problem in working on the imperative forms is that in the folk tales, the addressees of imperatives are always listed or traceable. In the elicited data, however, where many of the less common forms are found, the addressees are often not listed, thus making it sometimes impossible to pin down their exact meaning.

9.1. <u>ta</u>; male speaker to male addressee

eyąhį <u>ta</u>   'come!'   23-2

adǫxtu <u>ta</u>   'look!' (you all)   52-10

dątu ta   'you all take (it)!'   52-15

te yetu ta   'you all kill him!'   62-32

yąkutiki ta   'tell me!'   75-67

eki yąkǫ ta   'do so for me!'   89-94

kida ta   'go home!'   94-204

ku ta   'come back!'   160-2

There are a few instances where Dorsey glosses these ta imperatives as 'male to male, first time'. It is not clear what he meant by this: there are no instances of 'second time' imperatives, and indeed many imperatives are repeated over and over again in the tales with the same ta ending.

9.2. di; male speaker to female addressee

akanaki daca di   'come out and gnaw on it!'   29-28

dupaxi di   'open the door!'   33-8

umaki di   'go and bathe!'   34-31

ndao ku di   'come back here!'   95-231

nksponi dusi di   'grasp my ankle!'   96-247/8

o di   'shoot!'   127-2

9.3. te; female speaker to male addressee

dǫxtu te   'you all look!'   40-16, 18

dǫ te   'look at him!'   47-16

aksotu te   'you all make arrows!'   55-20

ahi te   'you all come this way!'   56-40

y̨axku daha <u>te</u>   'give it back to us!'   81-4

ku <u>te</u>   'come back!'   92-162

a <u>te</u>   'say!'   108-17

toho <u>te</u>   'lie down!'   109-34

9.4. **∅.** There are numerous imperative forms without an overt marker. Since the majority of these cases are from the second half of the corpus, it is impossible to tell who the speaker is and who the addressee is. Dorsey claims that these forms are used when addressing children (p. 3), and I suppose we will have to take his word for it. However, there is one clear instance where a female is addressing another female (76-46, 49), and there are others where children are addressed with the same forms used for adults (72-7, 113-19/20, etc.). I assume therefore that this is an optional manner of addressing children. It may well also be the usual form of females addressing females.

yaxkiduwa   'untie me!' (sun to child)   20-21

ndao hu ha̧ siniho̧ duti ha̧ca   'come here and eat mush
      with me!' (female to female)   74-46, 49

ihi akititu ya   'tell him to shut his mouth!'   138-24

de ha̧ kihaku   'go and get it for him!'   147-30

eke ya̧ko̧   'do so to me!'   157-14, 15

handa   'stay here!'   157-28

yuka   'you all stay here!'   157-29

yąxku   'give it to me!'   160-3

9.5. xye na, first person plural imperative.

te ye xye na   'let us kill her!'   150-18, 44-7

te ye ni xye na   'let us not kill her!'   150-19

kutiki xye na   'let us tell it!'   150-20

kutiki ni xye na   'let us not tell it!'   150-21

aku xye na   'let us feed him!'   150-22

akitupe xye na   'let us carry them on our shoulders!'

       150-23

atamini xye na   'let us work!'   150-24

Dorsey also lists eyą nkade xye (150-28) as an imperative:
'let us go there!'. Given the presence of the person marker, I
doubt that this is an imperative, and suspect that it means 'we are
going there'.

9.6.   na; second person strong negative imperative.
Person markers are used here:

yada na   'beware lest you all go!'   112-4, 8

ayį na   'do not drink it!'   142-35

itahi na   'do not run!'   142-36

yade na   'do not talk!'   142-37

yąhį na   'do not cry!'   143-1

akohi ine na   'beware lest you stand in the yard!'

      164-15

9.61. (<u>ku</u>)...<u>ni</u>. For less strong negative imperatives, the regular indicative forms are used:

> ayi̧ktu <u>ni</u> 'do not (ye) let him go!' 90-119
>
> akohi ina <u>ni</u> 'do not stand in the yard!' 93-184
>
> tuca ya <u>ni</u> 'do not touch it!' 93-189
>
> te hiya̧ka <u>ni</u> 'you must not kill me' 155-30

There is one instance where the person marker is omitted:

> ka̧ha̧ <u>ni</u> 'do not cry!' (Dorsey indicates that this is
>
> not a 'warning') 143-2

The remaining imperatives listed here are found only rarely in the Biloxi corpus. The examples of <u>hi ko</u> and <u>tki</u> are almost all from pages 160-161 of the <u>Dictionary</u>, which in itself points to their restricted use.

9.7. <u>hi ko</u>; the person marker is needed here. Since <u>hi</u> alone is a potential mode marker, perhaps <u>hi ko</u> is a sort of 'deferential imperative'.

> eke xyi di̧ ini <u>hi ko</u> 'well, why don't you walk (as you
>
> have been talking about it for so long!)'
>
> 160-29
>
> eke xyi di̧ io̧ <u>hi ko</u> 'well, why don't you make it (as
>
> you have been talking about it for so long!)'
>
> 160-32
>
> ayi̧xtu ikada <u>hi ko</u> 'you go home yourselves (instead
>
> of telling us to do so!)' 161-1

ayindi iku hi ko   'you come back yourself (instead of

     telling him!)'   161-3

ayade te xti ko yada hi ko   'you (pl.) have been so

     anxious to go, now go!'   161-20

xaxatu te xti ko,ixaxatu hi ko   'you (pl.) have been so

     anxious to stand, now stand!'   161-22

etikayǫtu te xti ko, etikayǫtu hi ko   'you (pl.) have

     been so anxious to do so, now do so!'

     161-23

9.8. dki ~ tki. In the introduction to the Dictionary (1912:3)
Dorsey claims that these forms are used by both males and
females addressing females. At present I see no conclusive proof
of this. Stems ending in -di drop the final vowel and add -ki.
Others add tki. There are very few examples of this form in the
data, and it may be significant that they are all preceded by
te xti ko.

     ayindi ded ki   'you go yourself!' (male to female)

       76-79

     yakide te xti ko, kided ki   'well, you go home (as you

       have been so anxious!)'   161-13

     ini te xti ko, nit ki   'well, walk (as you are so

       persistent!)'   161-15

yaki te xti ko, kit ki 'well, you carry it on your back (as you are so persistent!)' 161-17

yatoho te xti ko, toho tki 'well, lie down (as you are so persistent!)' 161-18

itahį te xti ko, tahį tki 'well, you run (as you are so persistent!)' 161-19

9. 9. ką. There are three examples in the corpus of ką used as an imperative marker. Dorsey claims that it is the form for female speakers addressing other females (1893:178). Unfortunately, in the two cases in which the identity of the people involved is known, the addressees are male. It may be important that in all 3 cases, 2 verbs are involved.

duxtą aku ką 'pull it and bring it here!' (old woman to son) 91-146

de dǫx ką cidike yuke 'go and see how they are!' (female to male) 92-164

nkpan ndǫx ką 'let me see and smell it!' 154-10 (interlocutors not identified)

Dorsey also claims (1912:205) that this form is used with verbs ending in -di, -ye, or -uni. This can only be a very ad hoc observation since neither aku or dǫhi, used above, fits that description.

9.10. ka̧ko. There are only two cases of this form in the data, and I suspect that they represent two morphemes (ka̧ + ko) rather than one. Again, Dorsey claims that it is used by males addressing males [he even specifies second time in his AAAS address (1893:178)], but I see no proof of it.

> witedi ewa ko ya̧, hu ka̧ko   'come day after
>
>   tomorrow!'   137-9
>
> yahede dawo hu ka̧ko,   'come hither now!'   137-11

9.11. There are a few other imperative suffixes that Dorsey lists in the Dictionary and in his AAAS address:

> tuki   male or female to female   'you too...'
>
>   (same as tki above?)
>
> tatka   male or female to male   'you too...'
>
>   (ta + tka?)
>
> tate   'female to male'

Since there are no examples of these forms in the entire corpus, I assume that they were obsolescent by the time Dorsey was collecting his data.

10. ha; the dubitative mode. Precedes: na/ni

The precise meaning of this mode is uncertain given the limited number of examples available. Like hi (see 3. above) it is found finally only in conjunction with the declarative na/ni. Unlike hi, however, it does not appear by itself in embedded sentences.

Examples:

        yihixtitu <u>ha</u> ni   'they might have the most'

              (fem.)   40-16

        cidike <u>ha</u> ni   'how would it be?'

              (fem.)   73-29, 31, 34

        etike <u>ha</u> ni, nkedi nixki   'I said it is so because...'

              (fem.)   76-87

        yahedi <u>ha</u> ni nkedi nixki   'I said this is the way

              because...'   (fem.)   92-154

        te hiye iyuhi <u>ha</u> ni   'you thought you killed her'

              (fem.)   94-205

        kiyetu ka̧ca <u>ha</u> na   'they must have told her'   95-233

11. Strong declarative mode:

              <u>xye</u>, masc. speaker   Follows: <u>dande</u>

              <u>xe</u>, female speaker   Precedes: <u>xo</u>

The semantic force of this mode seems to be stronger than that of the simple declarative mode <u>na</u>/<u>ni</u> (see 1. above).

Examples:

  <u>xye</u>:

        nitani <u>xye</u>   'it is large'   136-1

        yi̧ki <u>xye</u>   'it is small'   136-2

        anahi̧ asa̧ <u>xye</u>   'her hair is white'   136-9

nda dande <u>xye</u>   'I will go, whether he wishes or not'

137-22

ade ixyotu <u>xye</u>   'they talk very rapidly'   164-20

<u>xe</u>:

itoho ko nitani <u>xe</u>   'the log is large'   118-8

ti nopa xaxa maki ko cti <u>xe</u>   'the two standing houses

are red'   118-9

tohoxk atahi amaki ko kdexi <u>xe</u>   'the running horses

are spotted'   119-15

nkapa nedi <u>xe</u>   'my head aches'   136-3

<u>xye</u>/<u>xe</u> is sometimes followed by <u>xo</u> (see 6. above). It is not
clear whether there is any resulting change in meaning (see
especially the second example below).

ti ne ko sa <u>xye xo</u>   'the house is white' (masc.)

117-18

nda dande <u>xye xo</u>   'I will go whether he wishes or not'

(masc.)   137-22 (cf. above)

ewe yuke pa nitatani <u>xye xo</u>   'their heads are large'

(masc.)   136-5

kawa ksixtu <u>xe xo</u>   'they are very foolish or crazy'

164-16[2]

---

[2]Dorsey lists the speaker here as masculine. I think it must
be a mistake.

12. yeke marks an inferential mode. It is most frequently used together with a simple declarative marker:

Follows: dande

Precedes: na

anik wahetu yeke   'they must have gone into the water'   50-13

kide yeke na   'he must have gone home'   (masc.) 88-83

xohi dande yeke na   'it must be going to rain'   151-1

wahu dande yeke na   'it must be going to snow'   151-2

tayą kida dande yeke na   'he must be about to return' 151-6

hauti hąca yeke na   'he must be sick'   161-26

13. wa is a mode marking intensification. It seems to have a meaning similar to that of the superlative xti (see 15. below), although it is used far less frequently. It is not that xti is used for some verbs and wa for others, since they are both found with the same stems:

snihi xti   'it was very cold'   38-4

sni wa   'it is so cold'   149-21

yaǫ saha xti he   'she sang, making it very loud' 50-17

saha wa   'he was very strong'   46-12

Perhaps the glosses in the first two examples give us a clue to the difference between the two suffixes: xti meaning 'very' and wa meaning 'so'. Other examples are as follows:

> ahįske wa ande   'he was very greedy'   65-7
>
> kinepi wa di   'he is very glad'   71-6/7
>
> kinepi wa   'he is very glad'   88-68
>
> ksixtu wa   'they are very crazy'   113-22

wa is often glossed as 'always':

> nkaduti wa nkande   'I am ever eating'   149-26
>
> atamini wa kande ni   'he is not always working'
>
>   149-28
>
> nkatamini wa nkande ni   'I am not always working'
>
>   149-30
>
> ayade wa di   'you are always talking'   285a
>
> ayaduti wa di   'you are always eating'   285a

14. ǫ ~ ǫni, the completive mode. This mode is used to emphasize that the action of the verb took place in the past.

Follows: te   xti

Precedes: xa

ǫ:

> eyą̄hį̄ ǫ   'he got there (long ago)'   26-2
>
> atuka kitani ǫ   'the raccoon was first (in the past)'
>
>   26-9

kiye ǫ   'he said to her (in the past)'   33-8

nkaduti te xti ǫ   'I wished to eat (in the past)'   133-6

ndoxtu uxw ǫ   'our throats were dry'

   (='we were thirsty')   133-13

ǫni:

kitsąya yą tanaki utoho ǫni   'the American first lay in

   it (in the past)'   31-11/12

ąxti yą int ką ku ǫni   'he gave the woman to him (in

   the past)'   34-28

ąya de ca ǫni   'these people died (in the past)'   42-1

ani yą hu ǫni   'the water was coming'   50-8/9

ǫ is often followed by xa; the combination is sometimes glossed as
'regularly in the past' [which would be expected (see 635:7)] or
'in the remote past'.

ąya di o ca yixti ande ǫ xa   'a man was killing all the

   fish (in the past)'   33-1

amawo de ǫ xa   'he went to another land (in the remote

   past)'   33-6

kide ǫ xa   'she went home (in the remote past)'

   34-34

etikǫtu ǫ xa   'they did so (regularly in the past)'

   53-22

kokta de ǫ xa   'he went and ran off (in the remote

past)'   71-4

tao yuke ǫ xa   'they were killing deer (regularly in

the past)'   82-27

15. The superlative mode: xti.

This mode marker has been listed last because of its quasi lexical overtones, as opposed to the others which are purely grammatical. That is, its position within the verb is freer than that of other modes; rather than have a set position, xti immediately follows whatever it is intensifying.

Examples:

supi xti tu   'they are very black'   32-16

tca yi xti ande   'he was killing all'   33-1

eta nkǫ xti ni   'I do just so'   (fem.)   67-4

yande xya xti xyo   'you will always live, if...'   70-10

wahe xti   'she screamed exceedingly'   75-60

kįktu ni xti   'they did not let her go at all'   90-122

kupi ni xti ni   'it is so bad'   (fem.)   91-140

iyąsi xti   'you smell so strong'   108-5, 11

nkaduti te xti ǫ   'I wished to eat very much'

(='I was very hungry')   133-6

ti yįki xti   'the house is very small'   134-15

ikinitą xti   'it is too large for you'   134-17

xuxwe <u>xti</u> dande yeke na   'it must be going to blow

very hard'   151-4

The following are examples of <u>xti</u> with adverbs:

ewite <u>xti</u>   'very early in the morning'   19-5

kuhi <u>xti</u>   'very high'   26-8

yatana <u>xti</u>   'very soon'   70-9

įxyǫ <u>xti</u>   'very quickly'   160-1, 2, 3

There are a few cases in which 'very small' is written

y<u>į</u>k <u>sti</u> (112-10, 109-25, etc.) rather than y<u>į</u>ki <u>xti</u>. Since there are

no examples of y<u>į</u>k <u>xti</u>, I assume this shows a regular change of

x → s following vowel syncope.

700. Derivation

710. Nouns

There are two basic types of derived nouns in Biloxi:
nominalized verbs and compound nouns.

Nominalized verbs are formed by prefixing /<u>a</u>-/ to the
verb root.

Representative examples:

sǫ   'sharp at all ends'

<u>a</u>sǫ   'briar'   13-16

duti   'eat'

<u>a</u>duti   'food'   16-21

duksa   'cut with a knife'

aduksa   'woodrat'   39-2

wude   'burn bright'

awode   'sunshine'   54-1

kudexyi   'striped, spotted'

akudixyi   'letter'   207a

asne   'steal'

‖a + asne‖ → /asne/   'thief'   254b   (see rule 8)

cį̧   'be fat'

acįni   'grease'   264b

711.   Compound nouns fall into two categories: noun + noun, and
noun + verb. For the morphophonemic rules regarding
compounds, see rules 8 and 11.

Representative examples:

<u>noun + noun</u>

‖cindi + aho‖ → /cindaho/   'hip + bone'   'hip bone'

29-28

‖tą̧to + ahi‖ → /tą̧tahi/   'panther + skin'   'panther skin'

76-83

‖ peti + ti‖ → /petiti/   'fire + house'   'fireplace'

140-6, 7

‖ka̧xi + konixka‖→ /ka̧xkonixka/   'bee + bottle'

'hornet's nest'   206a

‖psi + aduti‖→/psaduti/   'night + food'   'supper'

248a

<u>noun</u> + <u>verb</u>

‖ so̧pxi + o̧ni‖ → /so̧pxo̧ni/   'flour + make'   'wheat'

22-3

‖ ina + toho‖ → /i̧toho/   'sun + fall'   'sunset'   52-2

‖ exka + naska‖ → /exkanaska/   'buzzard + long'

'long-necked buzzard'   95-240

‖ masa + i̧kte‖ → /masi̧kte/   'iron + hit with'

'hammer'   177a

‖ a̧yadi + ade‖ → /a̧yadiade/   'people + talk'

'language'   190a

‖ cake + pocka‖ → /cakpocka/   'hand + round'

'fist'   260b

‖ cake + xohi‖ → /cakxohi/   'hand + old'   'thumb'

260b

720. Pronouns

The personal pronoun <u>indi</u> has already been discussed under
inflection (see 621). Another personal pronoun is <u>i̧kowa</u>, which
is not inflected, but which denotes action done by <u>oneself</u>. (For
examples of its usage see 933.) A case can be made, I think, for

the personal pronoun root being in with two derivational suffixes:
-di to emphasize the subject or the object of the verb; -kowa to
underline that the action was done by oneself.

It is interesting to note that the reflexive pronoun -įxki-
(see 743. 4) would also fit this pattern (in + xki) except that it only
appears as a verbal prefix.

730. Interrogatives

731. Many interrogatives are derived from the prefix ca -. The
following is a partial list of them; morphophonemic rule 8
accounts for the vowel elision in some forms.

        cak ~ cakạ 'where? '   75-67

        cane 'where (stands)? '   93-196

        canaska 'how long? '   95-229

        cehedạ 'how high, tall, deep? '   123-13, 18

        cidike 'which, how, why? '   147-1

        cina ~ cinani 'how many? '   122-21, 22

732. Some pronouns have a derived form for interrogative usage:

        kawa 'something, anything'

        kawak 'what? '

        cina 'a few, many'

        cinani 'how many? '

740. Verbs

There are two basic types of verbal derivation in Biloxi: derivation of the root (including reduplication and compounding) and derivation of the stem (including thematic prefixes, dative markers, reciprocals, reflexives, and instrumentals).

741. Reduplication

Root reduplication is a fairly common phenomenon in Biloxi. It is used either to show intensification of the action or, more commonly, a distributive sense of that action. In polysyllabic roots, the final vowel is usually dropped before the reduplication, resulting in a CVCCVCV pattern. However, there are certain cases where only the first CV of the root is reduplicated, resulting in a CVCVCV pattern.

Examples:

cakcake   'he hung up a lot'   15-3;

      cake   'hang up on a nail or post'

tixtixye   '(his heart) was beating'   16-25;

      tix   'beat'

supsupi   'black here and there'   28-17;

      supi   'black'

soṣoti   'it is sharp at all ends'   43-9;

      soti   'sharp'

unakcikci   'he dodges all about'   44-8;

        kci   (?)

xoxoki   'he broke it here and there'   46-6;

        xoki   'break'

xoxohitu   'they are old'   49-1;

        xohi   'old'

cecehi   'it dripped off him'   52-11;

        cehi   'drip'

duxtuxtą   'he pulled them out (one after another?)'

        52-13;   xtą   'pull'

anixanixye   'he plays here and there'   61-5;

        anixye   'play'

kuku daha   'she gave to each of them'   67-5;

        ku   'give'

ixkidusasa   'she scratched herself often'   85-10;

        sa   'tear'

wudwude   'it lightened'   90-127;

        wude 'burn bright'; given as widwide in 52-12

ǫnacpicpi   'my feet are slipping'   153-33;

        cpi   'slip'

742. Compound stems

    There are two types of compound stems: noun + verb and
verb + verb. It is interesting that of the ten examples we have of

noun-verb compounds, only 3 are formed with a verbal root other than /ǫ/, 'do, make':

$$\| \text{ayą} + \text{į} + \text{duko} \| \rightarrow /\text{ayįduko}/ \quad \text{'tree + with + whip'}$$

'whip against a tree'   46-9

$$\| \text{ta} + \text{o} \| \rightarrow /\text{tao}/ \quad \text{'deer + shoot'} \quad \text{'shoot deer'} \quad 65\text{-}1$$

$$\| \text{he} + \text{e} \| \rightarrow /\text{he}/ \quad \text{'that + say'} \quad \text{'say that'} \quad 37\text{-}8$$

All of the others follow the pattern:

$$\left\{ \begin{array}{c} \text{noun} \\ \text{pronoun} \end{array} \right\} + \text{ǫ}$$

with three variations:

1. noun + y (glide) + ǫ

$$\| \text{aksi} + \text{y} + \text{ǫ} \| \rightarrow /\text{aksiyǫ}/ \quad \text{'arrow + make'}$$

'make arrows'   113-29

2. $\left\{ \begin{array}{c} \text{noun} \\ \text{pronoun} \end{array} \right\}$ + -k (obj. marker, see 934) + ǫ

$$\| \text{įdas} + \text{k} + \text{ǫ} \| \rightarrow /\text{įdaskǫ}/ \quad \text{'with back + do'}$$

'sit with one's back to...'   54-1

$$\| \text{ką} + \text{k} + \text{ǫ} \| \rightarrow /\text{kąkǫ}/ \quad \text{'string + make'} \quad \text{'trap'} \quad 86\text{-}30$$

$$\| \text{kawa} + \text{k} + \text{ǫ} \| \rightarrow /\text{kawakǫ}/ \quad \text{'what + do'} \quad \text{'what to do'}$$

93-190

3. $\left\{ \begin{array}{c} \text{noun} \\ \text{pronoun} \end{array} \right\}$ + ǫ

$$\| \text{cidike} + \text{ǫ} \| \rightarrow /\text{cidikǫ}/ \quad \text{'which + do'}$$

'which to do' (how)   44-1

‖amihi + o̧‖ →/amiho̧/   'summer, warm weather

+ make'   'have fever'   141-16

‖ha + o̧‖ →/hao̧/   'hominy + make'   'cook hominy'

142-13

Verb-verb compounds are as follows:

hane + o   /haneotu/   'they find and shoot'   17-31

kte + o̧ni   /i̧kteo̧ni/   'with + hit + do'   'to hit with'

176b

ayi̧ + naxE   /nkayi̧naxe/   'I + ? + hear'

'I ask a question'   195b

naxte + kide di   /naxtekidedi/   'kick + go home'

'kick and send flying'   224a

uxtaki + taho   /uxtaktaho/   'push + fall'

'to make fall by pushing'   224b

It should be remembered that morphophonemic rules 8 and 11 are optional for compounds. This explains why some compounds have two adjacent vowels and others have no vowel syncope where we might expect it.

743. Derivational prefixes

743.1. <u>Thematic prefixes</u> follow person markers (see 630) and precede dative markers (743.2) and instrumentals (743.5). Their meanings are not always easy to specify.

1. a- seems to have three basic meanings:

    a. habitual action:

        do̧ 'see'

        kado̧ ni 'he never sees' (=blind) 126-5

        duse 'bite'

        aduse 'he bites habitually' 127-16

        pxu 'gore'

        apxu ye di 'she gores habitually' 127-18

        naxte 'kick'

        anaxtetu 'they kick habitually' 128-10

    b. directional indicator: 'there, on'

        do̧hi 'look'

        ado̧xtu ta 'look!' (male to males) 52-10

        yihi 'think'

        ayihi 'he thought' 62-38

        noxe 'chase'

        akikinoxe 'they chased it one after another'

                88-77

        xehe 'sit'

        axehe ye 'he set it on' 90-114

kite   'shoot'

a̱kite   'he shot (there)'   95-220

ni   'walk'

a̱kini   'walking on them'   95-241

toho   'lie down'

a̱toho   'he laid on it'   109-27

c. transitivizer

hį   'arrive'

a̱hįtu   'they took her there'   50-15

kįhį   'arrive home'

a̱kįhį   '(they) took her home'   55-8

kuhi   'high'

a̱kuhitu   'they raised it'   95-239

2. į- instrumental prefix, 'with'. The forms here are given morphophonemically due to their relative complexity.

‖ ayą + į + duko ‖ → /ayįduko/ (8)   'tree + with + whip'

               'whip against a tree'   46-9

‖ į + das + k + ǫ ‖ → /įdaskǫ/   'with + back + obj. + do'

               'sit with one's back to'   54-1

‖ į + nixye ‖ → /įnixye/   'with + play'   'play with'

               87-64

$\|\,\xi + kte + \varphi ni\,\| \rightarrow /ikte\varphi ni/$ 'with + hit + do'   176b

$\|\,tasi + \xi + ca + ye\,\| \rightarrow /t\xi s\xi caye/$ (8)   'grass + with +

expend + cause'   'cut grass'

(also 'scythe')   176b

3. <u>u</u>-; 'within a given area'

yihi   'think'

<u>u</u>yihi   'he thought'   19-4

toho   'lie down'

<u>u</u>toho   'he lay in it'   27-2

kci   'dodge about'

<u>u</u>nakcikci de 'he went dodging about (the house)'

44-8

si   'step'

<u>u</u>si   'he steps in it'   71-6

xwehe ye   'set'

<u>u</u>xwehe ye   'she set it in'   95-237

wahe   'enter'

<u>u</u>wahetu   'they went into'   113-31

743.2. The dative marker <u>ki</u>- follows the thematic prefixes. Morphophonemic rule 7 accounts for the presence of /y/ in stems beginning with vowels.

kiyetu   'they said to him'   37-7

kidǫhi ye daha   'he showed it to them'   52-4

yąxkiyoxpa   '(they) drink it up for me'   69-4

ikikahį   'you tell about it'   70-9

yąxkiyotu te   'shoot at it for me!'   (female to males)

   85-3

kinitą xti   'it is very large for him'   134-16

axkidustu ni   'we did not take it from him'   141-28

ikipukta nąki   'you are sitting by him'   143-4

yąkipukta inąki   'you are sitting by me'   143-6

yakinaxtetu   'you (pl.) kick one another'   224a

kiduxtuki   'he pushed it for him'   4800:342:15

kiducadi   'he washed it for him'   4800:342:15

The following examples of ki- show that it is also used when the
direct object is either a body part   or an animal belonging to
someone: this is the so-called dative of possession.

kiduxtą   'they pulled his (tail)'   62-40

kihanetu   'they found his (tail)'   66-14

kidǫhi   '(they) saw his (shadow)'   91-132

kidǫhi   'she looked at her (head)'   94-207

įkikta dande   'I will hit your (horse)'   125-2

įkidusi   'I hold your (hand)'   125-4

te hikiye   'he killed your (dog)'   139-23

te hikiyetu   'we killed your (dog)'   139-26

Two peculiarities of ki- need mentioning at this point:

1. it is almost never used with ku, 'give'; indirect objects are an inherent feature of this verb.

2. when used with ǫ, 'do, make', it becomes kik- without assuming any meaning of reciprocity (see 743.3).

kikǫ daha   'he made for them'   31-2/3

kikǫtu   'they made for him'   37-6

yąxkikǫ daha   'you do it for us'   55-20

kikǫ   'she was making it for him'   109-25

Although the glosses here might lead one to expect kik- to be a benefactive prefix, this cannot be the case, since we find kik- only with the verb ǫ.

743.3. When reduplicated, kiki- assumes the meaning of reciprocity. Since any verb with this prefix must inherently be plural, the -tu plural marker is optional.

kikiyohǫ   'they were calling to one another'   56-31

kikidǫhi   'they were looking at one another'   56-39

akikinoxwe   'they ran after one another'   86-23

ca kikitu daha nanteke   'they nearly killed each other'

141-8[3]

ca yąkikitu nanteke   'we nearly killed each other'

141-9[3]

_____

[3]The root YE, 'cause' is mysteriously missing from these examples; I have no explanation for it.

743.4. The reflexive prefix

ịxki- is the reflexive form in Biloxi; it is found immediately following the person markers, although there are certain 3rd person cases where ki- is allowed to precede the reflexive. Morphophonemic rule 8 accounts for the form ịxk in stems beginning with a vowel.

Examples:

ịxkiyadu ye ande   'he was wrapping it around himself'

      66-13

nkịxkukade   'I speak to myself'   191a

yịxkukade   'you speak to yourself'   191a

hịxkukade   'he speaks to himself'   191a

nkixkiyạhị   'I love myself'   201a

yixkiyạhị   'you love yourself'   201a

ixkiyạhị   'he loves himself'   201a

nkixkiktetu   'we hit ourselves'   215a

yixkiktetu   'you hit yourselves'   215a

kixkiktetu   'they hit themselves'   215a

nkixkidicatu   'we wash ourselves'   260a

yixkidicatu   'you wash yourselves'   260a

kixkidicatu   'they wash themselves'   260a

I have no explanation for why the vowel is sometimes nasalized and sometimes not, although we have seen denasalization take place under similar circumstances in morphophonemic rule 5.

743.5. Instrumental prefixes are used to show by what means the action of the root was carried out. There are five main instrumentals in Biloxi, and traces of two residual ones. They are always found immediately preceding the root, and are as follows:

1. da-; 'with the mouth or teeth'

    dasi   'he (turkey) took it with his mouth'   37-3

    dauxitu   'they bite it off'   143-33[4]

    dadeni   'he did not chew'   144-13

    ndaksuki   'I bit it in two'   213b

    adaxke   'he gnaws'   221b

    dacpi   'he missed grasping an object with his mouth'

        267a

2. du-; 'with the hand(s), claws, etc.'

    iduwe   'you untie it'   28-12

    kiduptasi ye   'he caused it to become flat for him'

        32-16

    duca   'he washed'   32-17

    dusi   'he took it'   37-5

    adusudu ye   'she was singeing   39-5

    dustuki   'he grasped with his claws'   43-7

    dupaxi   'he opened the door'   52-6

    nducke   'I pull out'   55-23

---

[4] $V_1 V_2$ is probably allowed here to avoid ambiguity.

ducpi   'she dropped her'   56-38

duksetu   'they clean it up'   57-46

3. duk(u)-; 'by hitting or punching'

  dukxoxoki   '(they) knocked it to pieces'   113-31

  adukuxke   'he peels vegetables'   221b

  dukuxuki   'he crushed it by hitting or punching it'

         225a

  dukuputwi   'he made it crumble by hitting it'   250b

  dukuckati   'he mashed the fruit by sitting on it or

         hitting it'   265a

  spdehi dukucpi   'the knife slipped'   267a

4. na-; 'with the foot'

  naxte   'he kicked it'   13-13

  naksedi   'he broke (a stick) with his foot'   213a

  onaputwi   'I make an object crumble by kicking it'

         250b

  inackati   'you crush it with your feet'   265a

  nacpi   'her foot slipped'   267a

5. pa-; 'by pushing'

  paya   'she was plowing'   73-23

  pawehi   'he knocked them'   87-47

  nkpani   'I knock him'   90-118

  npaxtani   'I move an object by pushing it with a stick'

         223b

6. pu-; 'pushing or punching'

    pucpi   'he failed in pushing or punching'   267a

    given as a synonym for dukucpi

7. di-; 'by rubbing or pressing between the hands'

    diputwi   'he made it crumble by pressing it between

    his hands'   250b

    kixkidica   'he washes himself'   260a

750. Adverbs

Many adverbs are derived from connectives, pronouns, and verbs and particles. A partial list follows.

751. Derivation by prefix:

e-, 'and (?), the aforesaid (?)'

    ede   ‖ e + de ‖   'just now'   151-22

    ewa   ‖ e + wa ‖   'in that direction'   135-18

    ewitexti   ‖ e + wite + xti ‖   'very early in the

    morning'   19-1, 2

    ema   ‖ e + ma ‖   'right there'   61-6

ke- (?)

    kecana   ‖ ke + cana ‖   'again'   46-10

    kecumana   ‖ ke + cumana ‖   'again'   108-6

kuhi- 'high'

    kuhadi   ‖ kuhi + adi ‖   'upstairs'   150-2

<u>ndo-</u> 'hither'

    ndao   ‖ndo + ao‖ (?)   'hither'   95-231

    ndosąhį   ‖ndo + sąhį‖   'on this side of'   127-18

    ndoku   ‖ndo + ku‖   'back hither'   67-7

    ndowa   ‖ndo + wa‖   'this way'   56-40

<u>ewa-</u> 'there'

    eusąhi   ‖ewa + sąhi‖   'on the other side of'   252a

752. Derivation by suffix

  -wa   'locative ending'

    ewa   ‖e + wa‖   'in that direction'   76-82

    hewa   ‖he + e + wa‖   'that way'   196a

    kowa   ‖ko + wa‖   'further along'   149-8

    ndowa   ‖ndo + wa‖   'this way'   56-40

  -yą (?)

    extiyą   ‖e   + xti + yą‖   'at a distance'   34-31

    eyą   ‖e + yą‖   'there'   163-13

    heyą   ‖he + e + yą‖   'there'   56-31

    ndosąhįyą   ‖ndo + sąhi + yą‖   'on this side of'

        123-3

    yaheyą   ‖yahe + yą‖   'to a distance'   34-23

    yuwayą   ‖yuwa + yą‖   'toward her'   87-50

760. Connectives

There are various derived connectives in the data; all of them have at least one connective within them.

e̱-, 'and (?), the aforesaid (?)'

    ehạ   ‖ e + hạ ‖   'and then'   28-13

    ekạ   ‖ e + kạ ‖   'and then'   44-1

    eke   ‖ e + ke ‖ (?)   'and so'   112-11

eke, 'so' (eke itself is probably a derived connective, cf. above.)

    ekedi   ‖ eke + di ‖   'that is why'   37-10

    ekehạ   ‖ eke + hạ ‖   'and then'   89-97

    ekekạ   ‖ eke + kạ ‖   'and then'   74-39

    ekeko   ‖ eke + ko ‖   'well'   55-20

    ekẹonidi   ‖ eke + ọni + di ‖   'therefore'   40-28

770. Numerals

771. Cardinal numerals

For some reason, there are no numbers above 'four' in all of the texts and elicited utterances; in fact, there are relatively few numerical constructions at all in the corpus. The following list is taken from Smithsonian entry 4800:348, p. 97 ff and can be found under various headings in the dictionary. Morphophonemic rule 8 accounts for the vowel elision in the derived numbers.

sǫsa   'one'

nǫpa   'two'

dani   'three'

topa   'four'

ksani   'five'

akuxpe   'six'

nąpahudi   'seven'[5]

dąhudi   'eight'[5]

ckane   'nine'

ohi   'ten'

ohi sǫsaxehe   'eleven'   (='one sitting on ten')

ohi nǫpaxehe   'twelve'

ohi danaxehe   'thirteen'

ohi topaxehe   'fourteen'

ohi ksanaxehe   'fifteen'

ohi akuxpaxehe   'sixteen'

ohi nąpahu axehe   'seventeen'

ohi dąhu axehe   'eighteen'

ohi ckanaxehe   'nineteen'

ohi nǫpa   'twenty'

---

[5]Dorsey claims that '7' and '8' may be derived from ‖ nǫpa + ahudi ‖ 'two + bones' and ‖ dani + ahudi ‖ 'three + bones' (238b).

ohi nǫpa sǫsaxehe   '21'   ('one sitting on two tens')

ohi nǫpa nǫpaxehe   '22'

ohi nǫpa danaxehe   '23'

ohi nǫpa topaxehe   '24'

ohi nǫpa ksanaxehe   '25'

ohi nǫpa akuxpaxehe   '26'

ohi nǫpa nąpahu axehe   '27'

ohi nǫpa dąhu axehe   '28'

ohi nǫpa ckanaxehe   '29'

ohi dani   '30'

ohi dani sǫsaxehe   '31', etc.

ohi topa   '40'

ohi ksani   '50'

ohi akuxpe   '60'

ohi nąpahudi   '70'

ohi dąhudi   '80'

ohi ckane   '90'

tsipa   '100'

tsipa sǫsaxehe   '101'   ('one sitting on 100')

tsipa nǫpaxehe   '102'

tsipa danaxehe   '103'

tsipa ohi sǫsaxehe   '111', etc.

tsipa nǫpa   '200'

tsipa dani   '300'

tsipa topa   '400'

tsipa ksani   '500'

tsipa akuxpe   '600'

tsipa nąpahudi   '700'

tsipa dąhudi   '800'

tsipa ckane   '900'

tsipįciyą   '1000'   ('old man hundred')

ukikįke   'one half';   written twice in the texts as

        kįkįke   55-11, 56-36

772. Ordinal numerals are nowhere to be found in the corpus.
Even in the Smithsonian material they are surprisingly omitted.
On the page entitled 'Ordinal numbers' (in 4800:348, a booklet by
Powell of phrases to be elicited), Dorsey has crossed out the
English glosses ('1st, 2nd, 3rd, etc.') and inserted 'once, twice,
three times, etc.'. Such adverbial phrases consist of the verb
de 'to go' followed by the cardinal number:

de sǫsa   'once'   4800:348, 99

de nǫpa   'twice'

de dani   'three times'

de topa   'four times'

de ksani   'five times'

773. Multiplicatives are derived from <u>akipta</u>, 'to double' followed by the cardinal number:

        akipta nǫpa   'twofold'   4800:348, 101

        akipta dani   'threefold'

        akipta topa   'fourfold'

        akipta ohi   'tenfold'

        akipta tsipa   'one hundredfold'

CHAPTER III

SYNTAX

800. Introduction

Biloxi is a post-posing SOV language. Its tactic units include interjections (I), adverbials (A), subjects (S), objects (O), verbs (V), and connectives (C).

It must be stressed that we are at the mercy of Dorsey, Swanton and their typesetter in defining the major syntactic components which are phrases, clauses and sentences; all of our definitions are perforce based on their punctuation.

There are three types of phrases in Biloxi; they are as follows:

1. interjectory phrase: any $\underline{I}$ preceded and followed by a pause. (See 910 below.)

     tenaxi   'Oh friend!'   21-1

2. postpositional phrase: pp N $\genfrac{}{}{0pt}{}{(y\b{a})}{(de)}$ (See 922 below.)

     doxpe itka   'inside a coat'   139-6

3. noun phrase: any $\underline{S}$ or $\underline{O}$. (See 931 below.)

     ayek ita   'your corn'   139-1

Clauses may be either dependent or independent, sentences

either major or minor. They are discussed at greater length
under 1000 and 1100.

900.   The tactic units

    1. Interjections

The following are typical representatives of this class.

911.   Interjectory particles such as:

    1.   human cries:

        aci   'o no!'

        aci aci   'ouch!'

        he ha   'hello!'

        įda   'well!'

        ko   'oh yes!'

        m: 'oh!'

        nu: 'help!'

        ux   'pshaw!'

        xo xo   'oh! oh!'

    2.   animal cries:

        a: a: 'caw'

        pes pes   'cry of the tiny frog'

        taǫ   'cry of the squealer duck'

        tį   'cry of the sapsucker'

912. Vocatives

With three exceptions, vocative forms in Biloxi are unmarked:

koko   'O grandmother!'   19-16, 17

tenaxi   'Oh friend!'   21-1

koni   'O mother!'   29-27

kaxo   'Oh grandfather!'   76-84

cidikuna   'Oh Cidikuna!'   91-146, 156

takaka   'Oh younger sister!' (male speaker)   272a

The three exceptions are:

tata   'Oh father!'   170a

nyaxohi   'Oh wife!'   293b

nyaicya   'Oh husband!'   293b

tata is interesting in that the normal stem for 'father' is adi. nyaxohi and nyaicya, on the other hand, are noteworthy because they include the first person morpheme, and mean, literally, 'my old lady', and 'my old man'.

913. Within the corpus, interjections are used only at the beginning of quotes, as follows:

"aci!", edi   '"oh no!", he said'   13-18

"aha, nkiyandipi na"   '"yes, I am satisfied"'

(masc.)   24-9

"k̦axo, kawa ahi"　'''grandfather, what kind of skin?'''

　　76-84

"k̦oni, kupi ni xti ni"　'''Oh mother, it is so bad'''

　　(fem.)　91-139/40

"cidikuna, xapxotka y̦a duxța aku k̦a"　'''Oh Cidikuna,

　　pull down the empty box and bring it here!'''

　　91-146

"ko, y̦istitu ha x̦a"　'''oh yes! you are all scared,

　　eh?'''　93-175

"ux! șit kudi ni ha"　'''pshaw! that ugly boy!'''　109-31

920.　Adverbials

The following belong to the adverbial class:

1.　adverbial particles

　　tohanak　'yesterday'

　　em̦a　'right there'

　　ey̦a　'there'

　　kiya　'again'

　　y̦axa　'almost'

(see 750 for further examples)

2.　postpositional phrases

3.　a number preceded by de, 'go'

　　de n̦opa　'twice'

　　de dani　'three times'

　　de topa　'four times'

Although adverbials are most commonly found immediately preceding the verb, they can appear also before subjects and objects. They never follow verbs, however, and they never precede sentence initial connectives.

921. Adverbial particles

Examples:

skakanadi <u>ewitexti</u> ey̨ahi̧ yuhi   'the Ancient of Opossums thought he would reach there very early in the morning'   26-1

<u>ewitexti</u> exka pockana hane   'very early in the morning the buzzard found the old short one'   34-17

ekek̨a <u>kiya</u> dedi   'and then he went again'   46-6

<u>ndao</u> ku di   'come back here!' (male to female)   95-231

<u>tohanak</u> wahu   'yesterday it snowed'   135-3

922. Postpositional phrases. (See morphophonemic rule 8 for cases of vowel elision.)

1. <u>itka</u>   'in, among'

hawi<u>tka</u> de n̨aki dande na   'I will sit here among the leaves'   47-18

ti<u>tka</u> de ye   '(they) put him in the house'   112-10

doxpe <u>itka</u> xahe ye   'to put a bottle, etc., inside a coat'   139-6 ti <u>itka</u> de   'inside this house'   152-6

ti <u>itka</u> yą̧   'inside yonder house'   152-7

akutxyi <u>itka</u> yą̧   'under or within yonder book'   139-11

hama <u>itka</u> yą̧   'under or in the ground'   139-13

2. <u>kuya</u> ~ <u>okaya</u>   'under'

    ayahi <u>kuya</u>   'under the bed'   139-9

    yaxǫ <u>kuya</u>   'under the chair'   139-10

    aduhi <u>kuya</u>   'under the fence'   139-12

    itkap <u>kuya</u>   'under the board'   139-14

    yaxǫ <u>okaya</u>   'underneath the chair'   142-21

    aditǫ <u>okaya</u>   'under the table'   142-22

    ayahi <u>okaya</u>   'under the bed'   142-23

3. nata   'middle of'

    ani <u>nata</u> akuwe   'they came forth from the middle of

           the water'   50-15/16

    ani <u>nata</u> xti yą̧ ande   'she was in the very middle of

           the water'   56-32/3

    ti <u>nata</u>   'middle of a house'   153-20

    cake <u>nata</u>   'middle of a hand'   153-21

    akutxyi <u>nata</u>   'middle of a book'   153-22

4. <u>(u)wa</u>   'into, towards'

    asǫ<u>wą̧</u>[1]   'into the brier'   13-20, 139-27,28

---

[1]I have no explanation for the /ą̧/ here except perhaps overhearing.

ịkanạk <u>wa</u> de 'toward sunrise' 40-25

ịkanạki <u>uwa</u> de udunahi 'she turned towards sunrise'

   46-2

kusihị <u>wa</u> yạ 'towards evening' 158-15

pusi <u>wa</u> yạ 'towards night' 158-16

 5. yaskiya 'under' (I suspect this has a base form of

yaski, but I cannot confirm this because there is only one example

in the data.)

  ti <u>yaskiya</u> 'under the house' 139-8

 6. <u>yehi</u> ~ <u>yehi kạ</u> ~ <u>yehi yạ</u> 'close to'

  ani <u>yehi</u> da ọni 'he was going to the edge of the

    water' 75-62

  ani kyahọ <u>yehi kạ</u> 'close to the well' 13-8

  paxka isi <u>yehi kạ</u> 'the mole (was) close to her feet'

    73-23

  ani <u>yehi kạ</u> ịhị dixyạ 'when it arrived at the edge of

    the water' 88-85, 88-87, 89-89

  petuxte <u>yehi kạ</u> xex nạx kạ 'when she was sitting

    close to the fire' 109-28

  ayohi <u>yehi yạ</u> 'close to the lake' 50-7, 152-30-33

  inọni yandi yahi <u>yehi yạ</u> tox max kạ 'when her elder

    sister was lying close to the bed' 74-40/1

petaxti y̨ehi y̨ą toho hą   'and she lay close to the

       fireplace'   85-11

ani y̨ehi y̨ą j̨hj̨   'he arrived close to the water'

       94-213

7. acka   'near'

    axu acka xti   'by the stone' (very near)

       4800:348:219, 174b

    ąxu acka y̨ą   'near the stone'   4800:348:219, 174b

    ti acka y̨ą   'near the house'   174b

8. eusąhj̨ ~ sąhj̨   'beyond' (eu is a rare diphthong indeed;

but it is a shortened form of ewa, 'there')

    axu eusąhj̨   'on the other side of the stone'

       4800:348:219

    ąxu eusąhj̨ y̨ą   'on the other side of the stone'

       4800:348:219

    aduhi eusąhj̨   'on that side of the fence'   127-19

    ani tą sąhj̨ y̨ą hahi   'he brought him on the other side

       of the great water'   88-81

    yix sąhj̨ y̨ą de   'he went on the other side of the

       bayou'   112-12

    kudupi sąhj̨ y̨ąkudeska o di   'shoot at the bird at the

       other side of the ditch!' (male to female)

       127-2

aduhi s̱ạhị yạ   'on the other side of the fence'   127-4

9. ndosạhị   'on this side of'

    ạxu ndosạhị   'on this side of the stone'   4800:348:219

    aduhi ndosạhị   'on this side of the fence'   127-18

    yaduxtạ tạhị natkohi ndosạhị yạ   'on this side of the

        railroad'   252a

10. tawi   'on, on top of'

    ạxu tawi yạ   'on the stone'   4800:348:219, 270b

    pạhị tawi yạ   'mustache' (on top of the beard)   270b

    ti tawi yạ   'upon the house'   270b

11. ǫ ~ ǫha   'with'

    cakik ǫha ktedi   'he hit him with his hand'   13-10/11

    cakik ǫ ịkạhị   'he dipped up (blood) with his hand'

        113-39

    taneks ạyadi ade yǫ   'with the Biloxi language'   242b

922.1.   Almost all of the above postpositions seem to allow de or
yạ to follow them. de retains its usual meaning of 'here' or 'this'.
yạ is sometimes glossed as 'the' and other times has a quasi
demonstrative force to it, meaning 'yonder'.

922.2.   Postpositions used alone as adverbials.

    The following are examples of postpositions used without a
preceding noun. Their value becomes thus adverbial:

są̄hį yą̄ kiya nkǫ   'I do it again on the other side'

    13-13

są̄hį yą̄ kįhį   'he reached the other side'   86-38/9

są̄hį yą̄ de sįx ką   'when this one stood on the other

    side'   93-176

są̄hį yą̄ akanaki   'he got over to the other side'

    95-221

itka yą̄ ustki   'to stand a tall object in something'

    200b

itka yą̄ cudi   'to put a number of small objects

    (e. g. seeds) in something'   200b

kuya kedi   'to dig under, undermine'   217a

923. Some interrogatives

    1. cidike ~ cidiki   'how? why?'

how:

    cidike ha ni   'how would it be?'   73-29, 31, 34

    cidike de nkadi nani wo   'how can I climb this?' 89-95

    de dǫx ką cidike yuke   'go see how they are!'

        (said to child)   92-164

why:

    cidike ̣etikayǫ   'why do you do thus?'   19-10

    cidike kadeni   'why does it not burn?'   138-8

<u>cidike</u> iyąhį hi inąki wo   'why do you sit there

crying?'   146-17

<u>cidike</u> "kok ayudi" hecǫtu   'why do they call the

magnolia by that name?'   147-1

2. <u>cak</u> ~ <u>caką</u>   'where'

It is not clear what governs the choice between these two

forms. The difference is not phonological:

<u>cak</u> nąki hą   'where is the sitting (man)?'   121-5

<u>caką</u> nąki   'where is the sitting (pine forest)?'

121-18

Nor is it due to animate vs. inanimate subjects:

<u>cak</u> nąki hą   'where is the sitting (man)?'   121-5

<u>caką</u> mąki hą   'where is the reclining (man)?'   121-6

I assume therefore that <u>caką</u> is the base form and that it

alternates freely with <u>cak</u>.   Other examples:

<u>cak</u> tiduwi xa wo   'where does he usually land?'

33-12/13

<u>cak</u> ande ko yąkutiki ta   'tell me where she is!'

(male to male)   75-67

ąya xehe nąki ko <u>cak</u> nąki hą   'where is the sitting

man?'   121-5

<u>caką</u> ne kuǫni ko   'where he stood before starting

back hither'   166-4

cak ǫne xkuni ko   'where I stood before I started

back hither'   166-5

3. cina   'some, many'

This particle has a base form for indefinite use and a
derived form for interrogative use:

cina   'some, many, a few'

cinani   'how many?'

cina:

axok kiduni cina yįki da   'he gathered a few small

canes'   16-18

cina psohe cucuk max   'there were a few things piled

here and there in the corners'   40-18

cina ayoyuxtu ko dątu ta   'take as much as you (pl.)

please' (male to males)   52-15

koniška yą kutu dixyį cina ǫni ko henani xya nedi

'when they gave him the bottle, it had as

much in it as before'   70-7

cina nkoyihi ko ndą dande   'I will take as many as I

please'   153-31

cinani:

tohoxka ko cinani yukedi   'how many horses are

there?'   122-4

kšixka ko cinani yukedi   'how many hogs are there?'

122-7

cinan yuk nkyehǫ ni 'I do not know how many there

are' 122-11

There are a few examples of cinani where it does not seem

to be an interrogative. I have no explanation for this:

anahįk cinani kiduwe 'he untied some hair for her'

56-34

tą yįki yą ti cinani ko etike na bayus yą 'there are as

many houses in Lecompte as there are in

Bunkie' 122-21

tą yą aya cinani ko tą yįki yą aya e kunatu ni 'there

are not as many people in Lecompte as

there are in Alexandria' 122-22

930. Subjects and Objects

These two units will be discussed together because their

syntactic makeup (that of a noun phrase) is for the most part

identical. There is strong evidence that they are separate units

since ką, a nominal particle, is used only for objects (see 934

below). Otherwise what is valid for subjects is also valid for

objects.

931. Subjects and objects can consist of simple nouns (N) (see

610 and 710), but they can also be expanded in numerous ways:

1. they can include a verb (V)

2. they can include a nominal particle (np)

3. they can include a demonstrative pronoun (dp).

This can be abbreviated as follows: ^S_O: N (V) (np) (dp). There is no freedom in the order of these elements: a noun is always the first element, and the other elements, if present, follow in the order given above.

NP's in which the noun is a personal pronoun are defined as follows: NP: N_{pro} $^{(dp)}_{(np)}$

If the pronoun is any other type of pronoun, e.g. de, 'this', the NP consists solely of that pronoun.

Examples:

S: N	ąya... 'people' 57-46
O: N	ąya... 'people' (obj.) 155-27
S: N V	ąya xohi... 'the old woman' 44-6
O: N V	ąya sįhį ne 'the standing man' (obj.) 117-1
S: N V np	ąya xohi yą 'the old woman' 67-11
O: N V np	ąya dusi yą '(the one who) arrested the man' (obj.) 156-33
S: N V np dp	ąya sahi yą he 'the Indian, too...' 31-12
O: N V np dp	ąya xohi yą he 'the old woman, her' 87-45
S: N np dp	ǫti yą he 'the bear, too' 53-20
O: N np dp	ti yą he 'the house, too' (obj.) 72-5
S: N np	ąya di 'the person' 109-30

O: N np   ạya k   'man' (obj.)   71-4

S: N dp   ạya de   'these people'   42-1

O: N dp   tando he   'her younger brother, too' (obj.)   72-6

S: N V dp   ạya nọpa amạkide   'these two men'   127-5

O: N V dp   ạya tạhị andede   'this running man' (obj.)   126-17

S: N_{pro} nkindi   'I'   89-93

O: N_{pro} ayịt   'you'   136-19

S: N_{pro} np   nkint ko   'I'   55-12

O: N_{pro} np   int kạ   'her'   56-25

S: N_{pro} dp   nkind he   'I, too'   72-7

O: N_{pro} dp   nkind he   'me, too'   33-12

932. The above discussion takes care of the large percentage of S's and O's. In addition, four other possible expansions need be mentioned:

1. S's and O's involving <u>possession</u> often necessitate having two nouns. In these cases, the possessor is always named first, and np's follow the second noun.

     ạya anahị kạ   'people's hair' (obj.)   36-1/2

     ạya ca uxek   'people's fingernails' (obj.)   37-3

     ạya tik   'the man's house' (obj.)   71-3

tuhe tukani yandi   'Tuhe's uncle' (subj.)   85-1

aya iticya ti ya   'the old man's house'   86-43

ama tupe ka   'the ground's hole' (obj.)   92-171

2. In sentences whose verbs include reciprocity, S can expand to S S:

cetkana oti kitenaxtu xa   'the rabbit and the bear were friends to one another'   15-1

3. Additive phrases[2] (e. g. 'a cow and a horse') are formed by the juxtaposition of the two nouns followed by the np ya:

tohoxk wak ya ndoho   'I saw a horse and a cow'   289b

wak tohoxk ya ndoho   'I saw a cow and a horse'   289b

ayato axti ya ndoho   'I saw a man and a woman'   289b

ayato axti ya ahi hamaki   'a man and a woman are coming'   289b

This construction is relatively rare in the data; since it parallels the construction of possessed nouns (see 1. above), the first three sentences are conceivably ambiguous.

4. "Alternative" phrases[2] (e. g. 'a cow or a horse') necessitate having 2 N's within an S or an O as well. The nouns are followed by ha in this case, which does not otherwise function as an np. Here again, there are very few examples in the data, so it is impossible to tell if there are other ways of saying the same thing:

---

[2] See Charles F. Hockett. 1958. 185-6.

sįto sąki ha hanǫ   'is that a boy or a girl?'   129-21

tohoxk waka ha hanǫ   'is that a horse or a cow?'

129-22

taneks ąya di mamo ąya di ha hanǫ   'is he a Biloxi or

an Alibamu man?'   129-23

932.1.   S's and O's sometimes contain no N as such but instead

(A)   V np which functions as S or O:

te ye ande yąką įdahi yetu   'they sent for the one who

had killed him'   34-22/3

pusi adadi yuke ko yihixtitu ha ni   'those who gather

things at night ought to have the most'   40-16

xoxohi yandi įdadade   'the old people went to hunt'

50-10

933.   Pronouns

The following are examples of personal pronouns in context.

See 620 and 720 for more information on them.

nkint he eta nkǫ   'I do so, too'   22-2

nkindi nkǫni na xo   'I did it (in the past)'   62-38/9

ayint kunyikte ni dande   'I will not hit you'   136-19

ayindi yaxkte   'you hit me'   140-20

int ką kite   'he hit her'   94-202

ind he kidedi   'he too went home'   113-26

nkįxtu ko įkcatu ni 'we have not forgotten you' 21-2

nkįxtu he ąksi nkǫtu hi na 'we too must make arrows'
113-27/8

ayįxtu ikįhį hi ko 'you all be coming home
yourselves!' 161-5

ayįxtu itatu na 'it is yours' (pl.) 164-28

įxt he uci 'they too lie in it' 28-5

įxtu ǫtu nani xyo 'they must have done it' 150-16

933.1. įkowa is a pronoun used to denote action done by oneself:

įkowa atamini aduti yane 'you work by yourself and
find food' 31-7

įkowa įdahi otu ni 'they hunt by themselves and shoot
it' 55-19

įkowa kipude hinke 'I joined them (by?) myself'
140-15

įkowa putwi hide 'it crumbled and fell of its own
accord' 202b

933.2. kawa is an indefinite pronoun, whose derived form kawak
serves as an interrogative pronoun:

kawa:

kawa nkyehǫtu ni 'we did not know anything' 22-8

kawa nkakix kidi 'I have carried something home on
my back' 28-11/12

kawa xidi kohidi hu   'something strange comes from

     far above'   33-11

kawa katoho ni   'he was lying on nothing'   52-11

kawa pastuki nax ką   'she sat sewing something'

     73-22

kawak:

  kawak iye yande wo   'what are you saying?'   61-7

  kawak iyǫ yayukedi wo   'what are you (pl.) doing?'

     62-34

  kawak iyayukuni ha yu   'what did you roast before

     you came?'   112-14/15

  kawak etike   'what is that?'   128-8

  kawak ǫ ne di   'what is he or she doing?'   137-25

kawak is sometimes shortened to kak:

  kak iyǫ etike inąki ha   'what are you doing as you sit?'
     72-16
  kak iyǫ ini yande wo   'what are you doing as you

     walk?'   86-34

  kak cidike yaku   'what is the reason you have come

     back?'   108-10/11

933.3.   cidike sometimes serves as an interrogative adverbial

(see 923), but it can also be an interrogative pronoun as well:

<u>cidike</u> andede   'which of the two?'   26-4

tohoxka <u>cidiki</u> ande ita   'which horse is yours?'

131-24

kihaki <u>cidike</u> yukedi   'what kin are they?'   138-2

934. Nominal particles (np)

The nominal particles are numerous, and it must be admitted that their syntactic usage has defied precise explanation.

Among the most common are:

yą

di

yandi

ką

-k

yąką

ko

∅

The following sentences demonstrate the heart of the problem in that identical S's can be marked by different np's:

1.   edi ąya xohi <u>yą</u>   'said the old woman'   67-10/11

                 (for word order in this example cf. 1030

                 below)

      ąya xohi <u>yą</u> hux nąkedi   'the old woman was coming

         in the distance'   89-98, 107

ąya xohi y̨ą emą kidi ką   'when the old woman came

right there again'   93-176/7

2.   kiye daha ąya xohi (∅)   'the old woman said to them'

39-10

ąya xohi (∅) i̧kxihi hande   'the old woman was

laughing'   67-8

hux nąkedi ąya xohi (∅)   'the old woman was coming

in the distance'   90-116

3.   ąya xohi di ąya ca xti   'the old woman killed many

people'   44-1

4.   ąya xohi yandi yi̧ki ksowǫ   'the old woman raised her

sons'   39-1

kidi ąya xohi yandi   'the old woman came back'

91-141

The following sentences show that the same problem exists for 0's
as well:

1.   ąya xohi y̨ą te ye   'he killed the old woman'   44-2

ąya xohi y̨ą he dustu ką   'when they seized the old

woman, too'   87-45

2.   ąya xohi ką akuwe hą   'she was carrying the old

woman along and'   50-14

3.   ąya xohi (∅) kyehǫtu ni   'they did not know the old

woman'   44-6

ạya xohi (∅) tukpe   'he changed into an old woman'

44-2

Judging from these examples, we can make the following statements about the np's:

1. They do not distinguish animate from inanimate nouns.

2. They do not distinguish specific from generic nouns.

3. They do not distinguish human from non-human nouns.

4. They do not distinguish masculine from feminine nouns.

5. They do not distinguish topics from comments.

6. They are not classificatory with respect to shape.[3]

7. yą, yandi, and ∅ can be used for both S's and O's.

8. The choice of np does not depend on the position of the S or O within the sentence.

In the midst of such uncertainties, however, we can be reasonably sure about a few things:

1. ką, as well as -k, yąk, and yąką, are used only for O's. ką:

ani yįki nax ką eyįhį   'they reached the small (sitting) stream'   34-30/31

ạsuna acu ayihixti ką pawehi   'he knocked down a great deal of dried duck meat'   87-46/7

---

[3] cf. this function of equivalent particles in Ponka.

tidupi ne ką hane   'they found the (standing) ford'

      90-129/30

int ką kite te ye hą   'he hit her and killed her and'

      94-202

-k:

    anik dǫhi nedi   'he stood looking at the water'   50-8

    ek wata   'he watched it'   71-2

    ąyak ịsịhị xti   'he is very much afraid of the man'

      71-4/5

yąką ~ yąka:

    ąyaxi yandi ąxti yąka cetkanak ku ką   'when the chief

      gave the woman to the rabbit'   44-12/13

    ta xi yąką kiyotu   'they shot the mystery deer for

      him'   82-22

    ąsewi yąka akyąhi   'he took the ax from her'   94-202

yąk:

    tunaci yąk kidǫhi hą   'they saw his shadow and'

      91-132

    cį yąk xkida   'I gather the fat'   96-249

    ama yąk toho   'she fell on the ground'   109-35

2. With two exceptions, yandi is used exclusively for human

N's.

    xoxohi yandi indahade   'the old people went to hunt'

      50-10

sįto yandi ksix wadi dupax ką   'when the boy who was

very bad opened the door'   53-19

ayihį yandi kįhį hą   'the wolf people came home and'

62-27

edi ąya xi yandi   'said the chief'   82-24

axtu yandi kidi hą   'their father came home and'

112-11

The two exceptions are:

ani yandi xwitka xti ką   'as the water was very muddy'

31-14

cǫk ta yandi ąsuna duktax ką   'when his dog scared

them off'   86-30/31

3. ko is used in the following three definable situations:

when the N is a pronoun:

ayindi ko iyąkaku yą   'what you fed me'   16-22

nkįxtu ko įkcatu ni   'we have not forgotten you'   21-2

int ko akiya ade ye   'he was burning it behind him'

88-82

when the main verb of the sentence is stative:

ti ne ko są na   'that is a white house' (masc.)   118-1

ayą sįhį ne ko te di   'the standing tree is dead'   118-5

doxpe naske nąki ko sade   'the coat hanging up is

torn'   120-14

ayewi ko udunahi   'he faces the door'   136-20

when a question word is involved:

cak ande ko yạkutiki ta   'tell me where she is!'

    (male to male)   75-67

ạyadi mạki ko kawakọ te ạksiyọ hamaki wo   'what are

    those people wishing to do by making

    arrows?'   113-18/19

laci ko cehedạ   'how tall is Charlie?'   123-2

cina nkoyihi ko ndạ dande   'I will take as many as I

    please'   153-31

a subgroup here involves comparisons:

tạ yịki yạ canaska ko enaska bayus yạ   'Lecompte is

    as large as Bunkie'   122-15

kšixka nedi ko canaska ukikịke ko skane enaska na

    'this hog is half as large as that one'

    122-20

tạyạ ạya cinani ko tạ yịki yạ ạya e kunatu ni   'there

    are not as many people in Lecompte as

    there are in Alexandria'   122-22

ti ne ko dehedạ   'that house is as high as this one'

    123-6

In sum, the nominal particles remain the thorniest problem of Biloxi syntax.

935. Demonstrative particles (dp)

There are two common demonstratives in Biloxi: de, 'this' and he, 'that'. Technically they are pronouns, since they can be inflected (see 622) and since they can substitute for nouns:

> de yaxkiyoxpa te yukedi   'they wish to drink this
>
>   for me'   69-4
>
> de oxpa   'he swallowed this'   113-18
>
> he eya yakidi   'you reach home'   87-59

935.1. However, I have decided to treat them on the same level with np's since they are so often found at the end of S's and O's. In this usage they serve as reinforcers of the noun.

de:

> aya de ca oni   'these people died in the past'   42-1
>
> aya nopa amaki de   'these two standing (sitting,
>
>   reclining, etc.) men'   127-5
>
> ti itka de   'inside this house'   152-6

he:

> skakana he   'the Ancient of Opossums, too'   26-6
>
> oti ya he   'the bear, he too'   53-20/21
>
> ti ya he dusi   'he took the house, too'   72-5
>
> nkind he yandusi   'you take me, too'   72-7/8
>
> ind he aksiyo   'he too was making arrows'   94-212

935. 2. Along with <u>he</u> and <u>de</u>, <u>yą</u> should also be mentioned.
Semantically <u>yą</u> often has the value of 'that', although it usually
has a neutral meaning 'the'. Morphologically it is quite different
from <u>he</u> and <u>de</u> because it can never appear alone and is never
inflected. Since its usage often parallels that of <u>de</u>, perhaps a
few examples are in order:

> ąya sįhį ne <u>yą</u>   'that standing man'   126-8
>
> ąya xehe nąki <u>yą</u>   'that sitting man'   126-9
>
> psdehi nǫpa mąki <u>yą</u> indikta ni   'those two knives are
>
> not his'   129-9
>
> tohoxk nǫpa xaxa amąki <u>yą</u>   'those two standing
>
> horses'   4800:348:198+

940. Verbs

941. Simple verbs [as opposed to the causative construction (942)
and expanded verbs (943)] consist of an obligatory person marker,
root, and number marker, and the following optional markers:

Prefixes:

> thematic prefixes (see 743.1)
>
> reciprocals, dative markers, reflexives (see 743.2;
>
> 743.3; 743.4)
>
> instrumental markers (see 743.5)

Suffixes:

mode markers (see 635)

object markers (see 633.3)

Auxiliaries or classificatory verbs (see 941.1)

941.1. Auxiliary: (h)andE/yukE

The auxiliary in Biloxi is a defective verb: ande is used for the singular, yuke for the plural. By itself, it functions as the verb 'to be' or 'to stay': hande, 'he stayed here', 157-26. Together with another stem, it lends a durative quality to that stem. Auxiliary constructions are different from compound verb constructions (see 742) and expanded verb constructions (see 943 below) in that both the stem and the auxiliary are inflected. Examples:

ande

de ande   'he was departing'   44-9

i̜kane ye hande o̜di   'she was making him vomit'

(in the past)   46-1

i̜cpe daha ande   'he was laughing at them'   52-13

iduti ayande   'you are eating'   56-44

kawak iye yande wo   'what are you saying?'   61-7

nkao̜ te nkande ni   'I wish to make hominy' (fem.)

95-228

ndusi nkapunu <u>nkande</u> 'I hugged him or her' 150-7

<u>nkanda</u> dande 'I shall be so' 155-22

(see morphophonemic rule 1)

te ye <u>ande</u> 'he was killing' 156-32

yuke:

iduti <u>yayuke</u> 'you (pl.) are eating' 31-7

dǫhi <u>yuke</u> 'they were looking at it' 52-5

uxte <u>yuke</u> hą 'they were making a fire, and' 65-1

eyą kįhį <u>yuke</u> dixyį 'when they were arriving there'
65-1/2

wata <u>yuke</u> hą 'they were watching and' 82-21/22

tao <u>yuke</u> ǫxa 'they were shooting a deer in the past'
82-27

hetikayǫ <u>yayuke di</u> 'you (pl.) are doing just so'
154-25

hetąkǫ <u>nyuke di</u> 'we are doing just so' 154-26

The plural marker -<u>tu</u> is not needed with the stem since <u>yuke</u>
itself signifies plurality.

941.11. In the negative forms, usually the stem is negated:

kox <u>ni</u> yuke di 'they were unwilling' 28-7

kukuhi <u>ni</u> yuke 'they could not raise (it)' 55-24

kukikahį <u>ni</u> hande 'he was not telling about it' 70-11

nde <u>ni</u> nkande 'I am not going' 151-9

But there are two cases in which ni is found after the auxiliary:

atamini wa kande ni   'he is not always working'

149-28

nkatamini wa nkande ni   'I am not always working'

149-30

I suspect this is due to the fact that the negative form of atamini is atamini, due to morphophonemic rule 9. ni may thus be placed after the auxiliary to avoid ambiguity.

941.2. Classificatory verbs

There are five classificatory verbs in Biloxi which, in addition to denoting duration, also designate the position of the subject. They are:

nąki   'sitting'

mąki   'reclining', 'in a horizontal position'

ne   'upright'

hine   'walking'

ande   'running'

Although classificatory verbs can be used as independent stems (kuhik mąx ką, 'when it was lying high', 149-11), it is interesting to note that they often occur with roots that mean the same thing that they do:

xe nąki   'she is sitting (sitting)'   86-40

tox mąki   'he was lying (lying)'   52-11

sįhįx ne   'it was standing (standing)' 149-9

ąya ni hine ayehǫ ni   'do you know the walking

(walking) man?'   117-4

ąya tąhį yande ayehǫ ni   'do you know the running

(running) man?'   117-5

Although these verbs are used mainly with animate nouns,
there are occasional examples of nąki, mąki and ne being used with
inanimate nouns as well:

ani yįki nax ką eyįhį   'they reached the small (sitting)

stream'   34-30/31

ayą ade mąki   'the wood lies burning'   138-3

One other idiosyncrasy of these verbs needs to be mentioned
here: when used as auxiliaries, they are inflected for the 2nd
person, but not for the first.

See morphophonemic rule 5 regarding nąki and mąki.

1. nąki   'sitting'

kak ayǫk yąhi inąki wo   'what have you suffered that

causes you to sit and cry?'   68-16

pa kidǫhi nąki   'she sat looking at her head'   94-207

ptaskǫni nduti nąki   'I am sitting eating bread'

133-19

ptaskǫni iduti inąki   'you are sitting eating bread'

133-20

ptaskǫni duti <u>nǫki</u>   'he is sitting eating bread'

133-21

nke ni <u>nǫki</u>   'I have not said it (while sitting)'   158-29

2. <u>mǫki</u>   'reclining'

There are no examples of <u>mǫki</u> used in the second person, so it is impossible to tell whether or not it functions as the others do in this respect.

įdahi ye daha <u>max</u>   'he continually sent for them'

52-2, 3

naxe <u>mǫki</u>   'he listened (reclining)'   70-12

kinaye ni <u>max</u> kǫ   'when he did not move'   109-34

ayǫ ade <u>mǫki</u>   'the wood lies burning'   138-3

plural form: <u>mǫktu</u> ~ <u>amǫki</u>; see also 941. 21 below

dǫhi <u>amǫx</u> kǫ   'while they were looking at him'   52-12

akikahį <u>mǫktu</u>   'they were telling news to one

another'   70-12, 158-13

3. <u>ne</u>   'upright'

ta duxke <u>ne</u> kǫ   'he stood slaying the deer'   66-13

kawak iye i<u>nedi</u> wo   'what were you saying as you

stood?'   67-12/13

kuhi de te <u>ne</u> hǫ   'he stood wishing to go upward'

96-244

tǫsi wak duti <u>ne</u>   'the cow is standing eating grass'

134-4

nkįkxihi _ne_ di   'I am laughing as I stand'   134-6

plural form: _ne_; see also 941. 21 below

   ade _ne_ di   'they were moving'   50-11

4. _hine_   'walking'

   ąya ni _hine_ ayehǫ ni   'do you know the walking man?'

      117-4

   tohoxk ni _hine_ ko toxka xe   'the walking horse is

         gray' (fem.)   119-3

5. _ande_   'running'

   mani _ande_ yą   'the (running) wild turkey'   36-1

   ąya tąhį _yande_ ayehǫ ni   'do you know the running

         man? '   117-5

941. 21. Plural forms of classificatory verbs

   While _mąki_ and _ne_ have plural forms, none of the other

classificatory forms do. In fact, _hamaki_ serves as the plural

form for all five verbs. Dorsey sometimes writes this as _amaki_,

but I believe the two forms are identical. _hamaki_ is inflected for

all three persons.

      ąksiyǫ _yamaki_ wo   'are you all making arrows?'

         113-20/21

      ca hanke te _nkamaki_ na   'we wish to kill them'

         (masc.)   113-22

ąya nǫpa ci <u>hamaki</u> nkehǫ **ni** 'I know the two reclining

men' 117-8

ąya nǫpa ni <u>hamaki</u> nkehǫ ni 'I know the two walking

men' 117-9

ąya xaxaxa <u>hamaki</u> ayehǫ ni 'do you know all the

standing men? ' 117-12

ąya nǫpa tąhį <u>amaki</u> nkehǫ ni 'I know the two running

men' 117-11

tohoxk nǫpa nini <u>amąki</u> ko toxka xe 'the two walking

horses are gray' (fem.) 119-9

ptaskǫni duti <u>hamaki</u> 'they are sitting eating bread'

133-22

ptaskǫni iduti <u>ayamaki</u> 'you all are sitting eating

bread' 133-23

ptaskǫni nduti <u>nkamaki</u> 'we are sitting eating bread'

134-1

942. The causative construction

<u>YE</u>, the causative verb, combines with other stems to make causative constructions. It is different from compound constructions or expanded verb constructions in that the stem preceding <u>YE</u> is never inflected and <u>YE</u> always is.

Morphophonemic rules 1, 8, 10, and 13 are responsible for changes seen in causative constructions, as well as rules 14-24 for the person markers.

The third person forms are quite regular:

te ye   'he killed her'   44-2

kidǫhi ye daha   'he showed it to them'   52-4

de ye daha   'he sent them'   52-13

te xkiyetu   'they killed it for me'   139-17

te kiyetu   'they killed it for him'   139-22

de yǫke te   'he wishes to send me'   156-7

adukce yetu   'they make so much noise'   165-27

The first and second person forms are slightly different in that ha is inserted between the first stem and the person marker for YE. Morphophonemic rule 8 accounts for ha being reduced sometimes to h.

first person:

axehe hanke nǫki na   'I have stuck it in (as I sit)'
(masc.)   90-115

ca haxkiya dande   'I will kill him for him'   146-13

kakuduksa hinye ni   'I did not peep at you'   146-16

cece hinke   'I make it drip'   153-24

utoho hinya dande   'I will follow (your trail)'   157-24

adukce hanketu ni   'we do not make too much noise'
165-28

<u>second person:</u>

ca hiyetu   'you kill them all'   55-22

te hiyaxkiyetu   'you (pl.) killed my...'   139-18

nepi haye   'did you do it correctly?'   142-4

cecehi haye   'you made it drip'   153-25

te hiya ni   'you must not kill him'   155-31

de hiyake te   'you wish to send me'   156-8

adukce hiyetu   'you (pl.) make too much noise'

165-26

943. Expanded verbs

Expanded verbs consist of one obligatory verb and one or two optional verbs in the same person and number. Only the final stem of an expanded verb contains any suffixes.

V: V   hedi   'he said it'   13-13

V: V V   nko ikte xo   'I do it, I will hit you if ...'

13-11

V: V V V   hane dusi duxke   'he found her, took her,

and skinned her'   76-81

950. Connectives

There are two kinds of connectives, coordinating and subordinating:

951. Coordinating connectives

951.1. Clause final coordinating connectives:

        hą   'and'

       hąca   'but, and subsequently'

Examples:

       e <u>hą</u> kidedi   'he said, and went home'   15-2

       ǫti yandi įske <u>hą</u> yahe yą de   'the bear was scared

              and went away'   15-5/6

       cu <u>hą</u> kustuki   'he filled it and set it down before him'

              23-6

       ǫti yandi hedi <u>hąca</u> te ye te cetkana ką   'the bear said

              that, but he wished to kill the rabbit'

              16-23/24

       apad ǫ <u>hąca</u> kiya dedi   'she wrapped it up, and

              subsequently went on'   74-47

       nda dande <u>hąca</u> nde ni nkande   'I will go, but I have

              not yet gone'   151-9

951.2. Sentence initial coordinating connectives:

       ekeką   'and then'

       ekehą   'and then'

       ekeko   'well'

       eką   'well'

eke   'well'

ekedi̧   'that is why'

ekeǫnidi   'therefore'

Examples:

<u>eką</u> towe yą aki yą toho   'and then the Frenchman lay next'   31-12

<u>ekeką</u> wax ade ąyato yą   'and so the men went hunting'   39-2/3

<u>ekeǫnidi</u> ąya anitkak yuke xa   'therefore, there are people under the water'   50-18/19

<u>ekeko</u> ąksǫtu te   'well, make arrows!' (fem. to males)   55-20

<u>ekehą</u> kuhi yą adi   'and then, he climbed up there'   89-97/8

<u>eke</u> he eyąhi̧ hą   'well, she arrived there, and'   89-98/9

952. Subordinating connectives

All of these connectives are clause final, although they can never be sentence final. ką, 'when', is by far the most common of this group. A case can be made for ką being identical to the objectivizing particle ką (see 934).

de hed hą   (see 952.1 below)

dixyi̧   'when, if'

dixyą   'whenever, when, if'

ka   'when'

kne   'just as, as soon as'

ko   'when, as, since'

kike   'although'

xyeni   'although'

Examples:

yaxkica daha xyeni nkįxtu ko įkcatu ni   'although you
      have forgotten us, we have not forgotten
      you'   21-2/3

kiyetu dixyį   'whenever they said (that) to him'   50-3

ayohik sahi xti watatu kike kudǫxtǫ ni xti   'although
      they watched the pond for a long time, they
      saw nothing at all'   50-13/14

axikiye hande ką   'when he was treating him'   85-1

ani akuditu ką, tunaci yąk kidǫhi ...   'when they
      peeped down into the water, they saw his
      shadow'   91-131/2

ekedį pusi dixyą   'therefore, when it is nighttime ...'
      111-4

952.1.   de hed hą. This is a clause in itself, meaning 'this
finished   and'; it is used as a connective phrase, marking the
action of the previous verb as past perfect:

dukucke <u>de</u> <u>hed</u> hạ tumockanadi xaninati kde

    'when he had tied it, the Ancient of Wildcats

    rolled it along for some time'   27-4

duti <u>de</u> <u>hed</u> hạ, max kạ kidi   'after they had eaten,

    when they two sat, he came back'   31-5/6

itamino ye <u>de</u> <u>hed</u> hạ anahị yạ kidakacke <u>de</u> <u>hed</u> hạ

    'when she had dressed her (and) tied her

    hair for her'   73-36/7

1000.   The clause

Based on Dorsey's punctuation, the clause is any string of tactic units which includes all of the following properties:

1. It is both preceded and followed by a pause.

2. It contains at least one non-embedded verb.

3. It contains from ∅ to 2 subjects. (2 S's are in fact rare.)

4. It contains from ∅ to 2 objects.

5. It contains from ∅ to 2 adverbials.

6. It may contain one and only one clause final connective.

1010.   Dependent vs. independent clauses

Dependent clauses (dCL) are those ending in a subordinating connective (see 952). All other clauses are independent.

1020.   Although there is some freedom as to the order of the tactic units within a clause, certain tendencies are apparent:

1. S usually precedes O.

2. O almost always precedes V.

3. C is either clause initial or clause final.

4. A usually appears immediately preceding V.

The constituent structure of the clause can thus be summarized as follows:

CL: (C) (S) (O) (A) V (C)

Examples:

CL: V etu xa 'so they say' (= they say/usually) 68-23

CL: CV ekeha̦ wahe xti 'and then it screamed exceedingly'

      (= and then /it screamed/ very much)

      75-60

CL: AV kuhik ado̦xtu ta 'look up!' (male to males)

      (= up/look!) 52-10

CL: SV a̦ckana de kake ni 'the Ancient of Crows said nothing'

      (= crow/head/this/did not say it) 73-34/35

CL: OV a̦tatka cudetu 'they abandoned the child'

      (= child/they abandoned) 72-1

CL: VC e ha̦ 'she said, and' (= she said/and) 72-2

CL: CAV ekeha̦ i̦kana̦k wade udunahi 'and then he went towards

      sunrise' (= and then/sunrise/toward/he

      went) 40-25/6

CL: CSV ekeką yinisadi ayihi xti kjhį 'and then many
buffaloes came' (= and then/buffaloes/
they were very many/they came) 55-9/10

CL:COV ekeką tando he dusi 'and then, she took her brother,
too' (= and then/her younger brother/
that one/she took) 72-6

CL:CVC ekedį pusi dixyą 'therefore when it is night'
(= therefore/it is night/whenever) 111-4

CL:SAV paxexka na di kiya dedi 'the Ancient of Red-tailed
Hawks went again' (= Red-tailed Hawk/
head/the/again/he went) 56-35

CL:OAV akutxyi uksani hu yaxkiye 'you will send me a letter
very soon' (= letter/very soon/here/you
will send me) 21-5

CL:AVC eyą kidi hą 'and she got home' (= there/she got
home/and) 72-2

CL:SOV tohoxka ayeki duti na 'the horse eats the corn'
(= horse/corn/he eats it) 137-17

CL:SVC anacidi eyįhį hą 'the ghost came there and'
(= ghost/came there/and) 69-1

CL:OVC ahi yą kidusi hą 'she took the skin from her, and'
(= the skin/she took from her/and) 112-15/6

CL:CSAV   eką towe yą akiya toho   'and then the Frenchman lay

next'   (= and then/the Frenchman/next/he

lay)   31-12

CL:CAOV   ekąhą kiya yeki kicutu   'and they planted corn again'

(= and then/again/corn/they planted)   13-2

CL:CAVC   ekeǫniką nawunde uksi hande dixyį   'therefore, today,

whenever it is smokey'   (= therefore/

today/smokey/it is/whenever)   57-48/9

CL:CSOV   ekeką ąxti sǫsa ątatka nǫpa yedą   'and then one woman

took two children'   (= and then/woman/one/

child/she made two/she took)   42-1/2

CL:CSVC   ekiką ǫti yandi įske hą   'whereupon the bear was

scared, and'   (= whereupon/bear/the/was

scared/and)   15-5

CL:COVC   ekehą akidi xaxahi dusi hą   'and then she took an

insect with a rough body, and'   (= and then/

insect/rough skin/she took/and)   40-26/7

CL:SOAC   tuhe tukani yandi tuhe titka de ye   'Tuhe's uncle sent

him into the house'   (= Tuhe/his mother's

brother/the/Tuhe/into the house/to go/he

caused him)   85-1

CL:SAVC   anedi ti ci ne ką   'when lice were lying in the house'

(= lice/in the house/they were lying/

upright/when)   112-1

CL:OAVC   ịsu yạ kiya kihanetu hạ   'they found his teeth on him again'   (= teeth/the/again/they found his/ and)   61-16

CL:SOVC   ạya xohi di ạya ca xti kạ   'when the old woman killed many people'   (= person/old/the/people/ killed/many/when)   44-1

CL:CSOAV (theoretically possible, but no example has been found.)

CL:CSAVC ekeọnikạ yinisa ti ci nạki dande ọni xyeni   'therefore, although there were going to be buffaloes in the house'   (= therefore/buffalo/house/ lying/to be/ were/although)   52-18/19

CL:COAVC (theoretically possible, but no example has been found.)

CL:SCOVC eọnidi cọki cetkak noxe yuke dixyạ   'therefore whenever dogs are chasing rabbits'   (= therefore/dogs/rabbits/chase/they are/ whenever)   17-30/31

CL:SOAVC (theoretically possible, but no example has been found.)

CL:CSOAVC (theoretically possible, but no example has been found.)

1030. Position of S's and O's within the clause.

    1. Normally S's and O's precede verbs, as has been seen in 1020. However, there are numerous examples in the tales

where they follow the verb. Since there are no such examples in elicited data, I presume this was a stylistic device. It is almost always used after a quote when the speaker is identified. Moreover, the nouns involved are always animate.

Extraposed S's:

'aso̜ nki̜sihi xti" edi <u>cetkana di</u>   '"I greatly fear the

   brier", said <u>the Ancient of Rabbits</u>'   13-19

yecpi wadi <u>skakana di</u>   '<u>the Ancient of Opossums</u> is

   always lying'   26-15

eya̜hi̜ dusi <u>yi̜kadi yandi</u>   '<u>her husband</u> arrived there

   and took her'   75-76

tao yuke o̜ xa <u>a̜ya saha di</u>   '<u>the Indians</u> were shooting

   deer (in the past)'   82-27

Extraposed O's:

so̜sa kuku daha <u>ta ya̜</u>   'she gave one to each of <u>the</u>

   <u>deer</u>'   67-5

co̜k ta yandi dustu <u>int ka̜</u>   'his dogs seized <u>her</u>'

   90-121

Extraposed S and O:

"witedi ko eya̜hi̜ ta" kiye di <u>xyinixkaka pudedna di</u>

   '"Get there tomorrow!" said the <u>Ancient of</u>

   <u>Brants</u> to the <u>Ancient of Otters</u>'   24-11/12

2. S's usually precede O's , as stated in 1020. However, there are a few cases where this order is reversed. I presume that this was done for emphasis, and that the potential ambiguity involved was eliminated by a special intonation, or simply by context or by semantic probabilities.

> peska na kǫkǫ yandi axiki ye   'his grandmother shut
> up the Ancient of Tiny Frogs to make him
> mysterious'   46-1
>
> nahįte ątatka apux   'the child felt the moon person'
> 111-1
>
> tạsi tohoxka duti ne   'the horse is standing eating
> grass'   134-3
>
> ayek maxi yąki duti ne   'the hen is standing eating
> corn'   134-5

3. In the few sentences containing both a direct and an indirect object, the direct object is always first:

> ąya xi yandi ąxti yą int ką ku   'the chief gave him
> the woman'   34-27/28
>
> sǫsa ąckahǫ na ku   'he gave one to the Ancient of
> Crows'   39-1
>
> nasuki ąckahǫ na ku   'he gave the squirrel to the
> Ancient of Crows'   39-4/5

ąya xi yandi ạxti yạka cetka nak ku   'the chief gave

the woman to the Ancient of Rabbits

44-12/13

1100. The sentence

Since we do not know anything certain about Biloxi intonation,

we can only discuss the syntactic constituents of a sentence

according to Dorsey's own interpretation of it.

1110. The minor sentence (mSEN): any phrase (see 800) which

is preceded and followed by a pause. Here again, as with other

syntactic definitions, we are dependent on Dorsey's punctuation.

Examples:

kǫkǫ   'O grandmother'   19-16

ke   'nonsense'   24-19

xo xo   'Oh! oh!'   66-14

kudeska dahayi na ko   'the Ancient of Blue Darters'

57-49

ti yaski yą   'under the house'   139-8

tkana xohi   'old peaches' (= 'apples')   276b

1120. The major sentence (SEN): any construction containing at

least one independent clause, with optional minor sentences and

dependent clauses. There is never more than one minor sentence

in any given major one, and it always appears initially. There is

rarely more than one dependent clause; the final element within
any major sentence is an independent clause. Sentences
containing a dependent clause (dCL) are <u>complex</u>; those containing
more than one CL are <u>compound</u>.

SEN: mSEN

     pusi wa yą   'towards evening'   158-16

SEN: CL

     ekekạ acka na di kux nạke di   'then the Ancient of

            Crows was returning in the distance'   72-12

SEN: mSEN CL

     kọkọ, yạkataxni xti   'Oh grandmother, I am burned

            severely'   20-24/5

SEN: mSEN dCL CL

     kọkọ, xkitọ ni te nkande kike, cimana yạxkitọ ni ọkne

            'Oh grandmother, though I continually long

            to get there first, again he has gotten there

            before me'   19-7/8

SEN: dCL CL

     yaxkica daha xyeni, nkįxtu ko įkcatu ni   'although you

            have forgotten us, we have not forgotten

            you'   21-2/3

SEN: dCL dCL CL

     duti de hed hạ max kạ kidi   'when they had eaten, and

            while they were sitting, he came back'   31-5/6

SEN: CL CL

eyạ ahi hạ ạxti yạ kide di   'she reached there with

him, and the woman started back'   33-13/14

1130.   Embedded sentences

Embedded sentences are not overtly marked:

nyidǫhi nkahi nkihi na   'we thought <u>we were coming</u>

<u>to see you</u>' (masc.)   65-3

te <u>hiye</u> iyuhi ha ni   'you thought <u>that you had killed</u>

<u>her</u>'   94-205/6

ktǫhi yaǫ ac kạ   'when he asked <u>the frog to sing</u>'

96-244

ạtatka <u>ahị naxe</u> yihi   'he thought <u>he heard a child cry</u>'
                                                             118-18

<u>iduwe</u> nkihi   'I thought <u>that you untied it</u>'   145-4

<u>de</u> kukiyohạtu ni   'they do not wish <u>for him to go</u>'

165-11

However, in many cases the presence of a sentence medial
mode marker signals the presence of an embedded sentence. For
example, <u>hi</u> is a hortatory marker and as such is used when the
action of the embedded sentence has not yet taken place:

ịxt he uci dǫxtu <u>hi</u> kiye daha   'he told them that they

too should lie in it and see (how it is)'

28-5/6

ani ndǫ ni nkanda <u>hi</u> yihi   'he thought I ought not to

see water'   33-5/6

yao <u>hi</u> kiyetu ką   'when they told her to sing'   50-15

nko <u>hi</u> niki na   'I cannot shoot it' (masc.)

(= it is not that I can shoot it)   85-4

ąksi da ku <u>hi</u> kiye   'he told him to gather arrows and

come back'   85-15

ąxti nąkedi yakida <u>hi</u> edi na   'that woman sitting in

the distance says that you are to go home'

108-4/5

iduwa <u>hi</u> nkihi   'I think you ought to untie it'   143-31

isįhį <u>hi</u> nyedi   'I told you to stand up'   144-24

ndux ni <u>hi</u> yuhi   'he thought that I ought not to eat it'

144-26

ikici iku <u>hi</u> niki   'you cannot spare it'   (= it is not

that you can spare it)   159-10

da <u>hi</u> kiyuxtu   'they thought that he ought to go'   163-11

<u>ni</u> indicates that the action of the embedded sentence was not

carried out:

ita <u>ni</u> ikiyuhi   'they want you to die (but you will not)'

87-58

nkta <u>ni</u>'yaxkiyuxtu   'they wish me to die'   162-25 da ni kiyuxtu   'they wished him to go (but he did not)'

162-30

da ni kiyuhi   'he wished him to go (but he did not)'

163-2

wo indicates that the embedded sentence contains a very

mistaken idea:

etike nani wo yihi   'he thought it would not be so

(but it was)'   50-6/7

extixtik de di wo ayuhi   'he thought he had gone very

far (but he had not)'   61-13

tukanitu yą wo yihi   '(they) thought it was their uncle

(but it was not)'   65-2/3

atkyuhi toho hi wo yuhi   'she thought she would get

over him and lie down (but she could not)'

109-34/35

wo seems to have a variant form wi for embedded sentences:

uwe de dusi wi yuhi   'she thought she would go in and

catch him'   91-133

te ye wi yuhi   'he thought he had killed him (but he

had not)'   163-21

de di wi yuhi   'he (A) thought he (B) had gone'

(but he had not)'   163-22

ǫ ni wi yuhi   'he (A) thought he (B) had made it'

(but he had not)'   163-23

1200.   The following section contains diagrams of seven sample
sentences from the texts.   A free translation of these sentences is
as follows:

1.   The rabbit and the bear were friends to one another.

    15-1

2.   "I live in a very large brier patch, " he said, and went

    home.   15-2

3.   Therefore, whenever dogs chase rabbits, they find bears

    and shoot them.   17-30/31

4.   "Oh grandmother, though I continually wish to be first,

    he was first already. "   19-7/8

5.   When his nose could not get in (the dish), he could not

    eat.   24-16/17

6.   That woman sitting in the distance says that you are to

    go home.   108-4/5

7.   Our father wishes to kill us and sits making arrows.

    113-26/27

The top line of each diagram shows Dorsey's original
citation.   An interlinear translation follows, and the texts are
then given in phonemic, morphophonemic, and morphemic
notations.   The tactic units and their constructions are given
with the reference numbers to the section in which they are
discussed.

1. tcĕtkaná   oⁿ ti   kĭtĕnaxtu xa.

   (Rabbit/Ancient one)   (bear)   (friends to one another/used to be).

   /cetkana   ǫti   kitenaxtu xa./

   ‖cetka + na   ǫti   ki + tenaxi + tu + xa.‖

   {cetka + na + ∅   ǫti + ∅   ∅ + ki + tenaxi + tu + xa.}

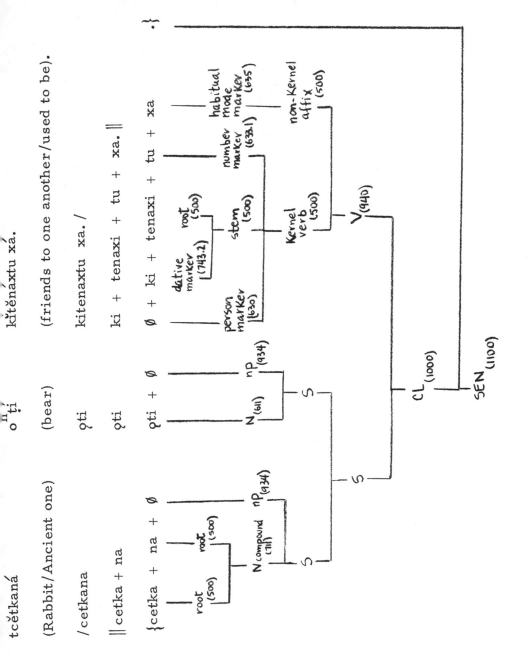

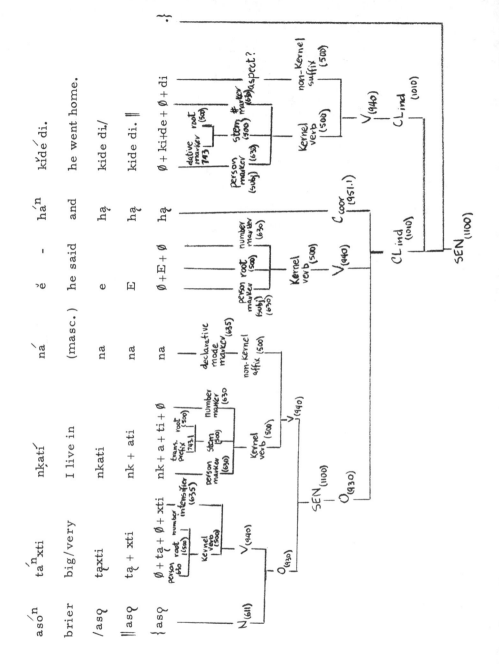

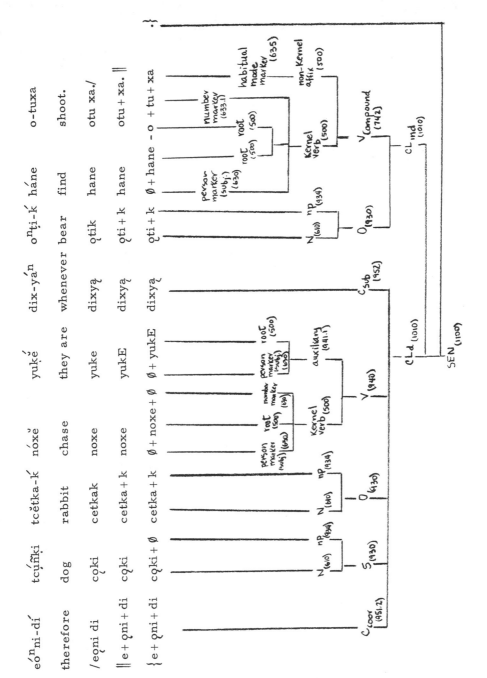

4.

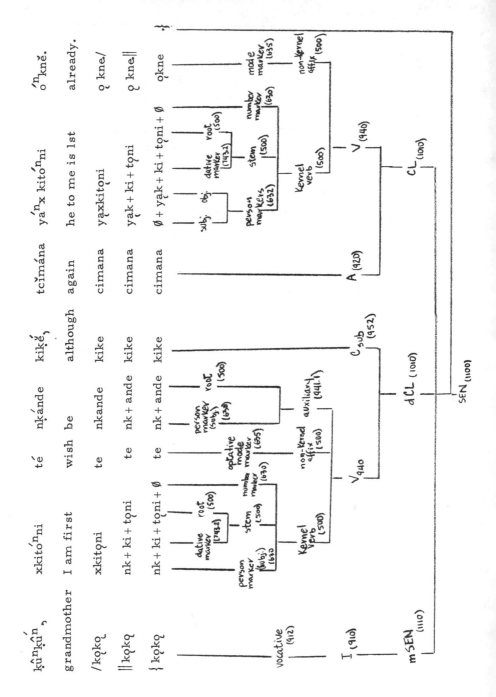

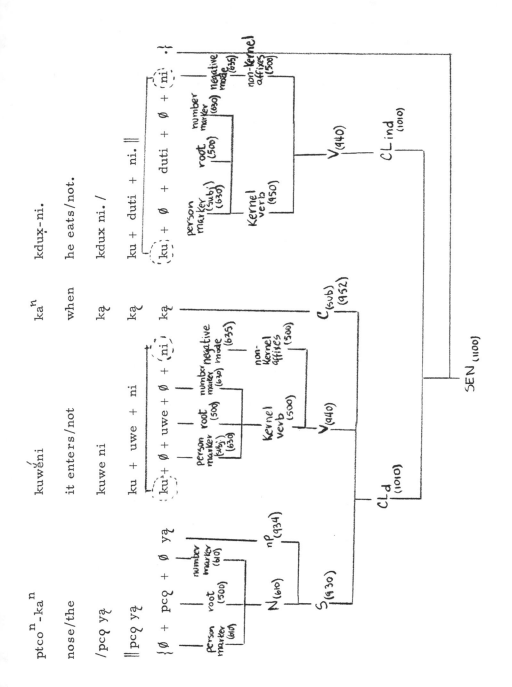

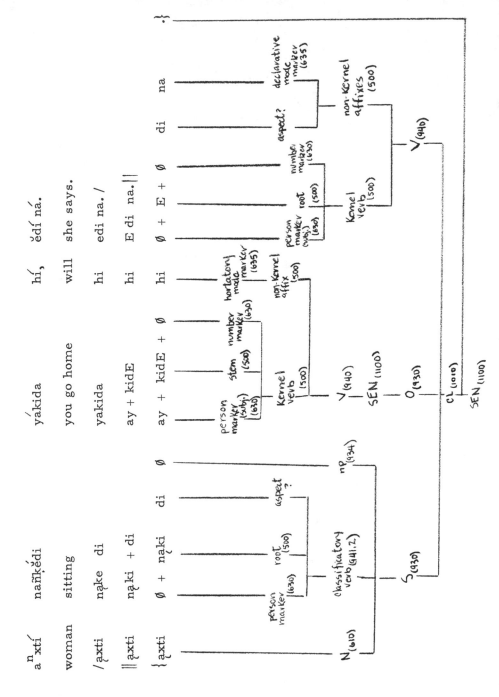

6.

aⁿxtí	nañk̇ědi	hí,	ědí ná.
woman	sitting	will	she says.
/ʒxti	nǫke di	hi	edi na. /
‖ ʒxti	nǫki + di	hi	E di na. ‖
}ʒxti	Ø + nakị	di	Ø + E + Ø	di	na

7.

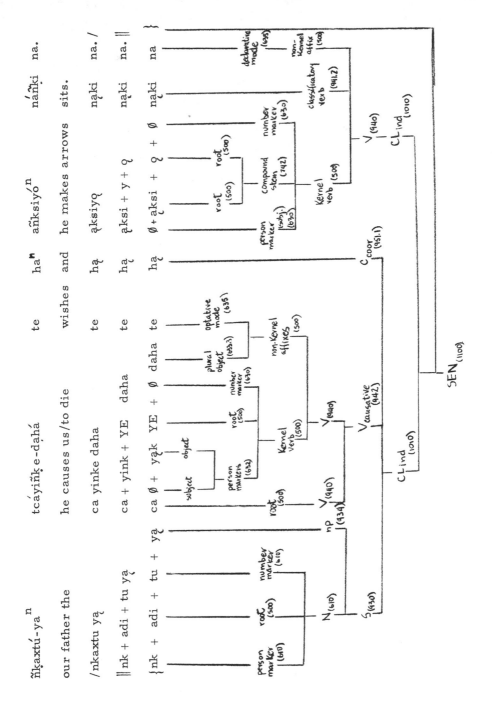

GENERAL BIBLIOGRAPHY

The following two bo oks were used for general purposes in writing thi s diss er tation. For the anno tate d bibliography of materi al available on Biloxi, rea d er s are advised to see section 050.

Hockett, Charles F. 1958. A course in modern linguistics. New York: Macmillan.

Powell, John Wesley. 1880. Introduction to the study of Indian languages. Washington: Government Printing Office.